Youth on Mission Volume 10

Christ Followers

A Year's Worth of Plans for the Youth on Mission Leader

Tonya Heartsill

Woman's Missionary Union®
Birmingham, Alabama

Woman's Missionary Union
P. O. Box 830010
Birmingham, AL 35283-0010.

Dewey Decimal Classification: 266.007
Subject Headings: Church Work with Youth
          Missions–Handbooks, Manuals, etc.
          Youth on Mission (WMU)–Handbooks, Manuals, etc.
          Religious Education–Youth
          Missions–Biblical Teaching

ISBN: 1-56309-869-5
978-1-56309-869-7
W046102•1005•1M2

Table of Contents

Youth on Mission How-To

Missions is all about joy. When you break it down, missions can be about praying, learning, giving, doing ministry, and witnessing—but it starts with the joy of God's presence in a person's life. That's why Youth on Mission® is an important part of your teenager's life. Through Youth on Mission, teens

❏ discover God in their everyday experiences
❏ go beyond the ordinary in their relationships with God
❏ experience God for Who He is
❏ are witnesses to God's faithfulness
❏ participate in God's awesome work in His world

What *joy* when young people connect with God's presence, power, and purpose!

Where does Youth on Mission fit?

Youth on Mission is a program of WMU. Youth on Mission is an approach to missions education for teenagers, grades 7–12, that enables them to nurture a dynamic relationship with God culminating in missions as a way of life for them. Youth on Mission is a vital part of the total youth ministry program in a church.

Youth on Mission isn't the name of a group, it is the goal. It's where we desire our young people to be—on mission with God. As they plan and participate in missions activities like praying, giving, Bible study, ministry and witnessing, they become Youth on Mission.

Who can be a Youth on Mission?

Any young person who is currently enrolled in grades 7–12 in school is eligible to be a part of Youth on Mission. If your church has a Youth on Mission organization, teens can join Youth on Mission simply by expressing an interest in belonging. Church membership is not required. In fact, Youth on Mission can include youth from the same church or from different churches in a community. The group can meet at the church, on a school campus, in a community center, or at a ministry site. You may even have multiple groups based on age, location, interests, or schedules.

If your church uses Youth on Mission material interjected into an ongoing aspect of your youth ministry program, teens can participate by virtue of their place in your total program. They will learn as they are exposed to the material in the context of growing Christian discipleship.

What about sixth-graders?

Youth on Mission is geared for young people in grades 7–12, and the materials are prepared for the abilities and characteristics of teens aged 12–17. However, churches often have to decide whether sixth-graders are "children" or "youth," especially

What's the Big Picture?

While missions programs will vary from church to church, many churches have the following missions organizations sponsored by WMU® and the North American Mission Board (NAMB).

Age Group	WMU	NAMB
Preschool	Mission Friends® (boys and girls)	
Elementary	Girls in Action® (girls)	Royal Ambassadors (boys)
	Children in Action℠ (coed)	
Youth	Acteens® (girls)	Challengers (boys)
	Youth on Mission℠ (coed)	
Adult	Women on Mission®	Baptist Men on Mission
	Adults on Mission℠ (coed)	

if the school system in their community includes sixth-graders in middle school. WMU recommends keeping sixth-graders with Girls in Action (GA), Royal Ambassadors (RA), or Children in Action when possible. It's important not to rush sixth-graders into becoming youth before they are ready. Churches should choose carefully for themselves if sixth-graders should be part of Youth on Mission.

Who leads Youth on Mission?

One or more adults help make Youth on Mission happen. Since Youth on Mission is for young men and young women, a balance of adult men and women leaders for an organization is ideal. Adult leaders form the Youth on Mission planning team and are available to the young people to listen, gather input from them, coordinate member responsibilities, and guide the work of the group. Obviously, the planning team also needs to work cooperatively and in a coordinated effort with the minister of youth or other youth leaders and the church's missions leaders.

But do adults do it all? Absolutely not! A good youth program has strong adult leadership. A *great* youth program includes youth in planning, coordinating, and organizing according to their interests, abilities, and skills. Delegate responsibility for specific projects, studies, or events to your Youth on Mission members. They learn and grow by being actively and integrally involved.

When do we meet?

As you've probably already noted, one of the great things about Youth on Mission is its flexibility. Youth on Mission can be an organization. Youth on Mission can be an emphasis within your total youth program. Youth on Mission can be your young people *on mission*!

If your church has a Youth on Mission organization, you may want to meet weekly. Certainly, there's more than enough material for your group in the Youth on Mission plan book. You might give time each week to a particular area, combining areas that seem to go naturally together. Or, you may make the missions project your focus each month and structure the weekly meetings in such a way that everything you do informs the project.

For Youth on Mission organizations, weekly meetings are a great idea, but Youth on Mission can be a once-a-month group meeting as well. A suggested approach to the monthly meeting is to have the missions Bible study coupled with a choice of one of the other key areas. If you follow this plan, we recommend that you choose a different area each month so as to interject variety into the experience. Over the course of the year, you'll want to give your teenagers different ways of looking at and being involved in missions.

Even greater flexibility is available when Youth on Mission is integrated in the total youth ministry program of your church. Elements from the Youth on Mission plan book can be interspersed into regularly-scheduled youth meetings, Sunday School classes, Bible studies, or other program hours, retreats, and the like. With the number of learning opportunities totaling well over 52, you can use one idea each week for the full year. You don't necessarily have to follow the plans in order. Choose the material that fits what your young people are studying in other areas of their lives and put a missions spin on the hot topic! In this way, you'll be making missions relevant to them.

Where are the curriculum plans?

The annual Youth on Mission plan book is your curriculum piece. It contains the entire curriculum you need for a full year. The Youth on Mission plan books follow an annual emphasis to provide a new look each year. The themes and "lesson plans" change from year to year because youth need variety and adult leaders do, too! However, they are undated material and can be used any year. And, no matter what theme they follow, each Youth on Mission plan book always covers the same areas:
- ❏ Bible study
- ❏ personal learning activity
- ❏ ministry and witnessing
- ❏ cultural experience
- ❏ missionary ministry

How do we use this resource?

Here's how the book is arranged:

Units 1–12

Introduction (for the leader)

Bible Study (plans for a one-hour session)

Learning Activity (plans for a one-hour session)

Ministry and Witnessing (plans for a one-hour session)

Cultural Experience (plans for a one-hour session)

Missionary Ministry (plans for a one-hour session)

Optional Activities (provide alternate activities for each of the five sessions in a unit)

Extra Pages

Contacts for Missions Trip Ideas

Helpful Addresses and Web Sites

Before starting, plan how you will use this book throughout the year. The units are not dated, so you can do them in any order you wish. It is suggested that you start with Unit 1 because it is the introduction.

Choose the sessions you will use each month. Each unit gives enough sessions for a Youth on Mission meeting each week for a month. Sometimes the sessions require planning a project to be done at another time. Make sure you check the church calendar and consult with other youth leaders before choosing a time for the project.

As you choose a session, check for any preparations that need to be made. It will help if you look ahead each month or quarter so you will be prepared with all supplies, speakers, etc. Knowing that materials will be necessary, be sure to work with your church to include Youth on Mission in your church's budget. Use your imagination to adapt material to meet the spiritual needs of the youth with whom you work. For supplemental missions videos to show during Missionary Ministry sessions, contact the International Mission Board or the North American Mission Board. (See "Extra Pages" for contact information.)

How important is planning?

Planning is key! As you plan, it's important to know what the point is. What are your goals for the young people in your Youth on Mission group? What is it you want to happen in their lives as a result of their involvement in Youth on Mission?

How to Use Youth on Mission Curriculum

Introduce Youth on Mission

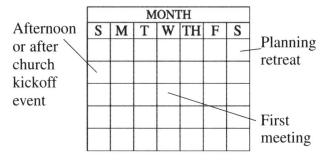

Weekly sessions

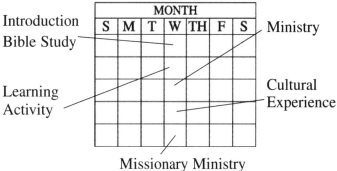

Months with only four Wednesdays*: plan to do Missions session on a Saturday

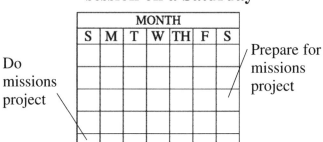

✓ To help you organize things, we've included a box for you to check as you complete each step before and during the session.

*Your group may choose to meet on a day other than Wednesday. This is just an example.

Hopefully, you have similar goals to those mentioned in the opening paragraphs on page v. If so, take time to reflect regularly on whether and how what you are doing is moving them toward those objectives.

Also, you'll want to consider at least three types of planning just to get the job done: yearly, monthly, and ongoing planning with your youth minister or other youth leaders. Yearly planning is the planning described in the previous section. Yearly planning involves sitting down with your adult planning team before the year ever gets started and taking a long view of the curriculum and projects for the year. You will want to coordinate planning with other missions leaders in your church. Chart out where you are going and the steps you'll take along the way to get there.

Monthly planning involves the adult planning team and any youth who are taking specific responsibilities for the month. For this planning session, the Youth on Mission plan book has everything you need. Decide what emphases you want to give to the curriculum for the month and who will do what. Briefly evaluate the previous month, asking, "What worked?" and "What do we need to do differently?" Briefly evaluate goals for the year to this point, too. Plan together how to make the current month the best yet!

If your church has a youth minister and/or a developed youth ministry program, keep in mind that Youth on Mission is a vital part of that total ministry. It is absolutely critical that you plan with your youth minister or other youth leaders. Before the year begins, discuss where and when your group will meet, *or* at what points Youth on Mission activities will be included in the youth program. On an ongoing basis, clear all dates and plans for special events through the youth minister and/or youth council, to ensure that you have a place on the church calendar and are not in competition with any other component of the youth program. Work together toward the annual youth missions trip (at spring break or during the summer). Demonstrate how Youth on Mission can assist in training for the missions project. Be willing to be involved in getting the teens ready to go!

How do I grow the group?

❏ Commit your leadership and the group to prayer. Seek God and His purposes for you and for the group. Trust Him to work.

❏ When it comes to attracting teenagers to anything, enthusiasm can't be beat! Be an enthusiastic leader. Your excitement will be contagious.

❏ Identify prospects. Within your church, youth Sunday School is a good place to look for prospects. Children's missions programs (GA, RA, and Children in Action) are also great places to start. Be intentional about helping preteens transition into Youth on Mission. Don't overlook youth in the school down the street or in your neighborhood, though. Your group may come from your community.

❏ Contact prospects. Use space in the youth or church newsletter. Make a call or write a note of invitation, for the personal touch. Involve teens in contacting and inviting other teens.

❏ Get the word out. Hang posters and distribute flyers throughout the church building or community. Produce a video of your teenagers doing missions and fellowshiping together; then, show the video at a youth event. Have a couple of young people share testimonies about being on mission—what they enjoyed and how it has influenced them and carried over into their everyday lives.

❏ More importantly, develop relationships with teenagers. Listen to them. Value them. Invite them into your home. Attend their extracurricular activities. Be available to them. Stay in touch with them. Your presence and attention communicates love and support.

❏ Start with a core group of teens, in your church or community. Give them your full attention. Pray for them fervently. Pour your life into them.

❏ Keep a notebook with information about each member. Note his or her address, phone number, email address, birthday, family information, school data, extracurricular interests and involvements, and spiritual development.

❏ Plan activities to build community. Find ways to make fellowships and events into ministry projects.

❏ From the beginning, include the young people in planning, organizing, and coordinating activities. Give them responsibility and permission to take the lead. Help them to have ownership in what they are doing.

❏ Always be willing to try fun, innovative ways of inviting and encouraging new members. Always be willing to try fun, innovative ways of getting your message across. Always be willing to try fun, innovative ways of being on mission!

How do we keep up with what our group does?

Records give insight into what's working and what's not, where things are going well and where they need to be adapted, who's involved at what level, and so on. Here's a sample of what you need to record:

1. Beginning of the year
    ❏ Objectives, goals, and calendar of events
    ❏ Structure of the group *or* plans for using Youth on Mission in the total youth program
2. Throughout the year
    ❏ Enrollment update
    ❏ Attendance at meetings and events
    ❏ Activities and projects conducted
    ❏ Evaluations
3. End of the year
    ❏ Accomplishment of objectives and goals
    ❏ Summary of enrollment and attendance
    ❏ At the end of the church year, give the church missions leaders or church clerk a report of your enrollment, attendance, and accomplishments for the year.

What other resources do Youth on Mission leaders need?

❏ WMU planning year book for the current year is an essential annual resource that gives a preview of study materials and special projects for the year, plus a complete list of resources for youth and information about other WMU ministries.

❏ The Youth on Mission section of the WMU Web site (www.wmu.com) is an interactive site where you'll find games, news from Youth on Mission groups, resources, leader helps, and more.

❏ Many other missions materials for youth, such as ministry idea books, spiritual growth helps, Bible studies, missionary biographies, and leisure reading materials are available. Order a free WMU Materials Catalog from WMU Customer Service, 1-800-968-7301 or view these products online at www.wmustore.com.

What else do Youth on Mission do?

❏ Ministry projects: Find ideas for ministry projects in the Youth on Mission plan book. Other projects may arise in response to needs in your community. Churchwide ministry projects may call for help from Youth on Mission groups. Often, Youth on Mission organizations like to work with the youth minister to include all youth in a ministry project. Remember to include time for planning and training, no matter what the project.

❏ Missions trips: Youth on Mission groups often participate in summer missions trips. For more information or to explore possibilities, contact WMU's Volunteer Connection at (205) 991-4097 or send an email to volunteerconnection@wmu.org.

❏ Special events: Associational and state Youth on Mission events can provide opportunities for youth from several churches to meet together for camps, retreats, or other activities. Churches sometimes plan ministry projects that youth can participate in together.

Missions is all about joy. When you break it down, missions can be about praying, learning, giving money, doing ministry, and witnessing— but it starts with the joy of God's presence in a person's life. May it be so in your life as you lead your youth to be on mission. God bless you!

Planning an Event, Activity, or Project

Title	Description	Date
		Time
Purpose	Goal this relates to	Place
Work to be done	Contact person	Phone number
	Others involved	Phone numbers
Leader/Participant training needs	Plans for training	Dates
Resources needed		Cost
		Budget available

Plans for:		Date to complete
Promotion/Publicity		
Decorations		
Room arrangements		
Other		

Plans for follow-up	Evaluation

Copy this form and use it to plan a Youth on Mission event.

Unit 1
Lost in a Lost World

Introduction
Which Way Should I Go?

Have you ever been lost? I mean the kind of lost where everything around you is unfamiliar. Where it is dark and raining and there are no street signs to tell you which way to go? It happened to me once; I vividly remember the day.

I was driving to a speaking engagement at a small country church in Kentucky. I had my map and specific directions about where I was to turn and what landmarks I should look for. I was confident I would find the church with ease. But, as the sun began to set and highway signs became harder to see, my confidence faded. Before I knew it, I was lost. At first it didn't bother me. I figured I would just turn around and go to the last marker on my map. I knew everything would be fine. I tried to convince myself there was nothing to worry about. But I never found the marker. Everything began to look the same. None of the highway numbers on my map matched the ones on the road. No doubt about it, I was lost.

Although I tried to remain calm, panic eventually set in. I remember stopping the car, pulling out the map, and staring at the road ahead. I had come to a crossroads. I had to choose which way to go. I closed my eyes, said a little prayer, and turned left. Within a few feet I saw it, a highway sign that had the number I was looking for! Relief flooded over me.

The feeling of being lost is one that no one enjoys. It is a lonely feeling of helplessness. That is how I imagine a life without Christ would be: lonely, helpless, and out of control.

In this unit, students will be challenged to think about a life without Christ. Some students may be struggling with questions about what the Christian life is all about. Some will feel they have heard the story one too many times. Challenge your youth to go deeper. If they are confident in their salvation, challenge them to seriously think about those they love who don't have a relationship with Christ.

It is time to bring Christ's love to our lost world. Let's not wait any longer to get started.

Bible Study
Fear Factor

Before the Session
❏ Gather the following supplies that will be used during the lesson:
  • One jar of pickled eggs
  • One jar of pickled pigs' feet
  (or something else equally gross)
  • Very ripe bananas
  • Markers
  • Colored pencils
  • Crayons
  • Dart
  • Prizes for those who participate in the opening activity
❏ Cut two 6-foot sheets of white bulletin board paper. Roll up and lay aside.
❏ Purchase a roll of wide black satin ribbon. Cut the ribbon in 8-inch lengths so each participating youth will have one.
❏ Read Romans 5:12–21 in several different translations.
❏ Set up a table in the front of the meeting room. Nicely arrange a silver tray with the pickled pigs' feet, pickled eggs, and ripe bananas on the table. Drape a sheet over the tray so the youth cannot see the tray when they enter the room.

- ❏ Make a sign on poster board with the title *Fear Factor* written in large, black letters. Place the sign in front of the table.
- ❏ Have a trash can and trash bags placed near the table.
- ❏ On poster board, draw a target of three rings. Label the outside ring, *Four Eggs*. Label the next ring, *Three Ripe Bananas*. Label the bull's-eye, *Two Pigs' Feet*. (The food items can be changed to anything that would be disgusting to teens.)
- ❏ Place a flip chart or chart paper at the front of the room. A marker board or chalkboard could also be used.

During the Session

- ❏ As students enter, invite them to come to the front of the room and sit in front of the table. Begin by telling them that for today's lesson, you are going to start with an episode of *Fear Factor*. Invite three volunteers, who claim to be fearless, to come forward. Play up the fact that this stunt should not be performed at home and that it has been tested by professionals for safety. Tell the contestants that if they complete the stunt, they will be named "Fearless" among the group and will be given a prize.
- ❏ Explain that the three contestants will have one stunt to prove their fearlessness. They will be asked to eat whatever is under the sheet. The number of items that they have to eat will be determined by the number they hit on the target with a dart. Unveil the food and show the group the target. Allow one of the onlookers to choose one of the three volunteers to go first. Have that person throw a dart at the target and attempt to eat the items. Continue this process with all three contestants. Provide a prize for those who complete the stunt.
- ❏ Bring the group back together in a circle and discuss what it means to be afraid. Have them define the word *fear*. Ask: *What is it? What causes it? How does it make you feel? What are you afraid of?*
- ❏ Make a list of common fears among children and youth. Write the list on a chalkboard or flip chart that can be displayed at the front of the room. Highlight two fears, fear of the dark and fear of death. Enlist a volunteer to read

Psalm 23:4 aloud. Ask: *What assurance does this verse give us?*
- ❏ Read the focal passage, Romans 5:12–21, to the group. Use a translation that is easy to understand. Compare and contrast what the Scripture says about Adam and Jesus.
- ❏ Form two groups. Give each group a sheet of bulletin-board paper and ask them to draw a mural. One group will be assigned a mural that depicts life with Christ. The other group will draw a mural that depicts life without Christ. Give students 10–15 minutes to work on their murals.
- ❏ Tape the murals on the wall and have each group explain what they drew and why. Use this time to share what it is like to live a life without Christ. Relate it to living in the dark. If possible, share a personal story at this time about your own experience of living without Christ in your life.

Close the Session

- ❏ Have the group come back to a circle formation. Hand out a black ribbon to each student. Explain to the students that this ribbon represents their friends and family who do not know Christ. Encourage them to put the ribbon in their Bibles or in a place where they are reminded to pray for those who are living in the dark.
- ❏ Instruct the group that you will close in prayer. Tell the students that during prayertime, you will ask for them to say the names of those who do not know Christ. Begin the prayer. Allow a few moments during the prayer for students to interject the names of those whom they want to pray for. End the prayer by asking God to touch the lives of those people whose names have been mentioned, that they would come to know Him soon.

Optional Activity

(In place of *Fear Factor*)

Before students enter the meeting room, turn off the lights and black out the windows to make the room totally dark. Have several flashlights hidden around the room. Have the students find the flashlights in the dark. As they find them, allow the students to turn them on. After all of the flashlights have been found, ask the students to describe what it felt like to be in the dark. Ask them if they were afraid at any point and what it felt like when someone finally found a flashlight and turned it on. Compare this activity to living in darkness without Christ. Compare the students to the light of the flashlight. Read Matthew 5:14–16.

Learning Activity
Follow the Leader

Before the Session

❏ Determine an area where "follow the leader" could be played while students are blindfolded. The area can be indoors or outdoors. If you choose to do the opening activity indoors, make sure you have notified other people that you will be using the facilities for your activity.

❏ Obtain a copy of the CD *Life, Love, and Other Mysteries* by Point of Grace.

❏ Arrange to have several adult volunteers help during this activity. If possible, assign a volunteer to every four participants.

❏ Have a bandana available for every student.

During the Session

❏ Tell the students you are going to lead them on a Sherpa walk. Explain to the students that when people decide that they will attempt to climb Mt. Everest, they hire a Sherpa, a local person familiar with the area and needs of climbers, to lead the way. Sherpas may not speak the same language as their followers. Explain that during this activity, each of the adult volunteers will be like a Sherpa. They will be leading their group through a course without communicating with them verbally.

❏ Give each student a blindfold to put on. Have the students get in a single file line with their hands on the hips of the person in front of them. Instruct the Sherpas to place themselves around the students so they can help them navigate through the course and keep the students from any danger.

❏ The youth leader should serve as the head Sherpa. Tell the students that the head Sherpa will be leading by making different sounds and

movements. It will be up to the students to listen closely and decide what each sound means. After a while, the students will catch on to the sounds and will follow accordingly. The volunteers will also need to use the same signals as the head Sherpa so they can help students through the course. It will be important that none of the adults give instructions verbally. If the students want to talk to each other, that is acceptable.

❏ Here are some sounds and actions that would be appropriate:

• Humming, while the lead Sherpa holds the hand of the first person in line and pulls gently—walk slowly

• Humming very quickly—walk quickly

• Hissing with a pat on the head—get down low

• Clicking sound while touching the student on the back of the knee—pick up your feet

• Barking while gently pushing on their back to get them down on their knees—crawling

❏ The head Sherpa should lead the group through several areas where the students will need to bend down, climb steps, walk over objects, crawl through a tight space, etc. Be creative with the activity. Allow 20 to 30 minutes to complete the course.

❏ After the activity is finished, ask students to tell where they went on the course. Have them explain what it felt like at the beginning when they didn't understand anything that they were supposed to do. Give students time to share how they felt. Allow volunteers to share how it felt for them to communicate only through sounds.

❏ Read Luke 9:23. Emphasize the part of the verse that says, "follow me." Ask several volunteers to explain what that means to them. Take a few minutes to share what the term *Christ follower* means to you. Explain that to be a Christ follower, you must seek God's direction and guidance throughout your daily walk. Use this time to explain the importance of spending time reading and studying the Bible.

Close the Session

❏ Have the students spread out around the room where they can be by themselves for a moment. Play the song "Any Road, Any Cost" by Point of Grace. Encourage students to think about the words of the song as it is played.

❏ When the song has ended, tell the students to take a few moments to pray about their own walk with Christ. Ask them if they are willing to go wherever God leads and do whatever God asks at any cost.

❏ Close the session by leading in prayer for the group as they learn to become strong Christ followers in their families, communities, and school.

Optional Activity

During the debriefing activity, invite a missionary to share his or her call to the missions field and the struggles he or she faced in service. Have the missionary share what it is like to follow Christ with no fear of what God will ask or where God will lead.

Ministry/Witnessing
Day of Ministry

Before the Session

❏ Contact a local homeless shelter, Christian Women's Job Corps® site, or other local ministry helping those living in poverty. Ask if your Youth on Mission group can host an event for the people with whom the ministry works. Set up a time when the group can host the event.

❏ Enlist adult volunteers to help during the event. One adult per five students is advisable.

❏ After setting up an event location, decide what your group will do. Determine the supplies that will be needed for the event. Ask church members for donations. Purchase any supplies that are not donated.

❏ Invite the director of the ministry where you will be serving to come and share with the students what to expect from the people they will encounter during the event. If the ministry requires any training before the event, make sure you provide that training for the students who will participate.

During the Session

Some event ideas:

❏ Sports day—Set up this event at a local park or open field. Include organized games, such as softball, volleyball, and soccer, as well as fun games like tug-of-war, dodge ball, and a water balloon toss.

❏ Country fair—Provide country music and fair games. Have a cake walk, ring toss, pin the tail on the donkey, golf putt, and go-fish games set up around the room. Provide hot dogs, chips, and cupcakes for participants. Use hay and corn stalks to decorate.

❏ Dessert party—Provide dessert and entertainment for the crowd. Have youth perform songs, skits, and puppet shows.

❏ Movie night—Select a favorite movie that entire families would enjoy. Set up a big screen TV, and serve pop popcorn. Give out licorice and Junior Mints during a time of intermission.

❏ Day of Hope—Plan a day when people in the church and community can donate their services to the homeless. Services might include free haircuts, dental checks, blood pressure checks by your local Baptist Nursing Fellowship chapter, personal hygiene items given away in packs, manicures, etc. Be creative with the services you provide!

❏ Day camp for kids and moms—Plan a day of fun and games for kids and a day of crafts and pampering for mothers. Provide lunch for the participants.

❏ Board Game Night—Gather various board games. Provide snacks and prizes for the winners. Play music and Christian videos during the event.

Close the Session

❏ No matter what activity you choose, build in time to introduce your students and share the reason your group is there.

❏ Prepare a short devotional or testimonial from a student and close the time in prayer.

❏ If possible, provide each participant with a small gift to remember the event.

Cultural Experience
Hide and Seek

Before the Session

❏ Write the following statistics on separate strips of paper and hang them around the meeting room. (Statistics from www.windyouth.org/mp_facts.htm, 2004)

- *23% of homeless teens are pregnant*
- *50% of homeless teens are escaping violence in their family homes*
- *93% of homeless teens are using drugs and/or alcohol on a regular basis*
- *79% of homeless teens have been sexually abused and/or assaulted*
- *25% of homeless teens are engaged in "survival sex" or prostitution*
- *40% of homeless teens have been living on the streets for over 6 months*
- *30% of homeless teens are robbed, beaten or otherwise exploited while on the street*
- *15% of homeless teens are second generation homeless*
- *32% of homeless teens have attempted suicide*
- *71% of homeless teens have been in foster care, group homes, or other youth institutions*
- *65% of homeless teens battle clinical depression and/or other mental health issues*
- *The average age homeless teens enter prostitution is the age of 14*

❏ Designate an area to play hide-and-seek.

❏ Purchase a backpack that will be given away to a homeless youth.

During the Session

❏ Play a game of hide-and-seek. Divide the large group into three smaller groups. Assign each group to be a "hider," "seeker," or "helper." Instruct the group that the hiders will hide and the seekers will seek. The helpers will help the hiders make their way back home without getting tagged. To begin, instruct the seekers to count to 100 and the hiders to find a place within a designated area to hide. After counting to 100, the seekers can begin looking for the hiders. The helpers will need to be on the lookout to help the hiders get back to home base. The helpers must also avoid being tagged by a seeker. If tagged, helpers lose their voices. They are still allowed to help the hiders, but they can no longer speak. The hiders must make their way back to home base without being tagged by a seeker. If they are tagged, they must freeze in their position and remain there until a helper unfreezes them. Continue to play the game until everyone has made it home or for about 15 minutes. If time permits, switch roles and play again. (Adapted from *World Changers Express,* Vol. 3, p. 101.)

❏ While the students rest, explain that for homeless youth, every day is like a game of hide-and-seek. Homeless youth hide from adults, police, and people who are out to harm them. They seek food and shelter. They constantly look for help from someone who is trustworthy, but that help is rare.

❏ Ask students: *If you were a missionary, what would you do to minister to the needs of homeless youth in America?*

❏ List the answers students give on a chalkboard, marker board, or flip chart.

❏ Ask: *If you were to find out that there was a homeless teen in your school, what would you do to help him? What could our group do to help him?*

❏ Read 1 John 3:17–24 aloud. Ask a volunteer to explain the verse in her own words.

❏ Take a few minutes to have the group brainstorm ideas about how they can help the homeless youth of today. Encourage youth to think of practical things the group could do. If you live near a metropolitan area where there are homeless youth, you may be able to volunteer at a youth shelter. If you live in a rural area, your group may decide to collect supplies and send them to a shelter. Encourage students to be creative as they think of ways to minister to homeless youth.

Close the Session

❏ Show the backpack you purchased. Challenge the group to bring an item to your next meeting to put in the backpack that would benefit a youth in your community who lives with the effects of poverty. Allow a few weeks to collect items for the backpack. Contact your local high school or middle school office and ask the staff to give the backpack to a deserving student. Ask the staff to keep the name of the donors anonymous.

❏ Ask each student to take one of the statistics off the wall and bring it back to the circle. Go around the circle, and have each student read the statistic. Ask for a volunteer to pray for the teens in America who face poverty and homelessness every day. Pray that your group will become aware of people around them who struggle with poverty and will find ways to minister to them.

Missionary Ministry
Michael Daily (Church and Community Ministries, Miami, Florida)

Before the Session
❏ Mount a world map on the wall or bring a globe to the meeting

❏ Pack a backpack with the following items: one orange, T-shirt, toothbrush, aspirin bottle, book, and small baby doll

❏ Become familiar with Michael Daily's information in During the Session so that you can share it in your own words.

❏ Check out a Cuban or Hispanic music CD from the library to be played as students enter the room

❏ Make Cuban Sugar Cookies to serve during the meeting:

During the Session
❏ As students enter, put them in various sized groups. Each group will represent a family. Some groups may have three people in them while others may have six or more. Tell the students that they are now a family unit. Give them ten minutes to decide what their family would need to take with them if they were moving to Mexico and all they could take would be what they could get in a van. Have them make a list of the essential items that would be needed.

❏ After each family has shared their list with the whole group, explain that this scenario is a

---

CUBAN SUGAR COOKIES

1½ cups shortening
1½ cups sugar
¼ teaspoon salt
2 egg yolks
½ teaspoon fresh lime juice
1 teaspoon real vanilla extract
4½ cups flour (more or less)
2 egg whites beaten with 1 tablespoon water

Preheat oven to 325ºF.

Cream shortening and sugar with an electric mixer. Add salt and egg yolks, blend. Add lime juice and vanilla. Continue beating, adding flour gradually until the mixture is stiff, but not too dry. Mix well.

Roll the dough into a cylinder about 2 inches in diameter. Slice the cookies about ½inch thick. Place on a greased cookie sheet. Brush cookies with beaten egg white. Bake about 25 minutes or until lightly browned. (www.icuban.com/food)

---

reality for migrant workers who have to come to the US to provide for their families.

❏ Explain that today, you will be telling them about Michael Daily who is a church and community ministry director in Miami, Florida. Direct the students' attention to the map (or globe). Show the students where Miami, Florida, is located. Point out the following countries on the map: Mexico, Cuba, and Haiti. Mark these countries by putting a red sticker dot on each one. Pull out the prepared backpack. As you pull out each of the following items, tell how they relate to the story of Michael Daily and his work in Miami.

Orange—More than 165 countries are represented among the population in Miami. Many of these people come looking for work. Many migrant farm workers move to the area because so much farming goes on all year long. Migrant workers move from place to place according to where the crops are in season. They are hired at minimum wage to harvest the crops. One of the crops harvested is oranges.

T-shirt—Due to the poor living conditions and low wages among migrants, some area churches have decided to help by collecting clothing and giving it away to the migrant workers and their families. Churches have also collected Christmas gifts for the children during the holiday season.

Aspirin—Michael Daily's wife, Ana, runs the Good News Care Center that provides free health care to those who have no health insurance. The purpose of the center is to meet the physical needs of individuals and then share the gospel to meet their spiritual needs.

Toothbrush—Michael also works with the mobile dental van that is owned by the Florida Baptist Convention. Michael works with area elementary schools to recruit patients who need dental care. The van parks at a local church and distributes New Testaments and health care kits to the patients who come.

Book—Explain that when migrants move to the US they usually don't know the English language. Many children learn the language quickly by going to school and interacting with other children, but adults don't have that opportunity. Michael helps coordinate literacy classes for adults so that they can learn the language and communicate their needs with others.

Small baby doll—Explain that one severe problem in the area is with 13–15 year old girls wanting to get pregnant. Many of these young girls have helped to raise their younger brothers and sisters and they feel that taking care of their own child would be easy. Since girls don't always receive emotional support and love from their families, they look to a child to provide that for them. Michael works through the Good News

clinic to help educate these girls about the reality of having a child at such a young age. He works with doctors in the community to provide education about the negative physical, moral, and emotional problems that a young girl can face upon getting pregnant at such an early age.

Close the Session

❏ Pass around the Cuban cookies for the group to enjoy. Explain that this is a Cuban treat that many migrant workers enjoy.

❏ Have the group sit in a circle. Share with them the following prayer requests to pray about during prayertime:

• Pray for the Good News Care Center and the work that they do with migrants.

• Pray for abstinence education for teenaged girls.

• Pray for opportunities to reach children for Christ through tutoring ministries.

• Pray for the mobile dental van and the people who take part in that ministry.

Unit 2
What's a Christ Follower?

Introduction
An Invitation to Join the King

The invitation arrived in a beautiful red envelope with a golden seal. It was personally addressed to me in lavish handwriting. At first, I hesitated to open it. Who was sending me such a stunning invitation? I didn't know anyone getting married, graduating, or expecting a baby. My curiosity got the best of me. I carefully peeled the seal off the back so that I wouldn't tear the envelope. The invitation was printed on creamy white paper that felt like satin. The background was a faint picture of a beautiful meadow. The paper shimmered in the light. The invitation was engraved in elaborate gold letters that read:

The honor of your presence is requested
at the table of the King.
Come as you are
there is nothing to bring.

I was shocked. The King wanted me to join Him for dinner? How could that be? I wasn't anyone special. As a matter of fact, I considered myself to be downright ordinary. I wasn't famous or wealthy. There was nothing about me that would stand out to the King, yet He invited me. Now it was my decision to attend.

In this unit, students will hear Scripture that points to salvation. They will receive their invitation to the feast. It will be their decision whether to accept the invitation.

Bible Study
Sacrifice

Before the Session

❏ Read through the story, "The King's Son," and become familiar with the content.

❏ Purchase a twin flat sheet and write the name *Jesus* in large, bold letters in the middle of the sheet with a fabric marker.

❏ Collect a variety of colored fabric markers to be used during the worship time.

❏ Ask a youth or adult to play worship songs on a guitar during the worship time. If no one is available to play guitar, select several worship songs from CDs that can be played during the worship time.

❏ Have several Bibles available.

❏ If you are not comfortable with sharing the gospel presentation one on one with a student, ask a volunteer (youth pastor, Sunday School teacher, deacon, pastor) to be available during the worship time to respond to youth who may be seeking salvation.

❏ Have a CD player available to use during the session.

❏ Find a copy of one of the following songs "King of Glory" by Third Day (*Third Day Offerings: A Worship Album,* Essential Records) or "Secret Ambition" by Michael W. Smith (*The First Decade: 1983–1993,* 1993 Reunion Records).

❏ Read through the verses that will be used during the session. Become familiar with what you should say after each verse is read.

During the Session

❏ Ask students to sit in a circle on the floor. Tell them you will tell them a story about a king and a prince. Ask them to listen closely. Read or tell "The King's Son" (p. 16).

❏ At the end of the story, ask a volunteer to read John 15:13 aloud. Ask a volunteer to tell what the Scripture means to them. Say: *Although "The King's Son" is a fictional story, it is true that a man has laid down His life for your sins. His name was Jesus. He lived among the people and became their friend. He laughed with them, cried with them, and ate with them. He loved the people so much that He chose to die in their place. He loves you, too. He wants to laugh when you laugh, cry when you cry, and share your life with you.*

❏ Ask a volunteer to read, Romans 6:23. Ask someone to tell what the Scripture means to them. Say: *We all sin. We do it every day. Even if we try to be perfect, we are going to sin. It is our nature. According to this verse, the penalty of sin is death. But, Jesus offers us a gift; the gift of eternal life. All we have to do is accept the gift.*

❏ Ask a volunteer to read (or quote) John 3:16. Say: *In this verse, we are told why Jesus gave His life for us; because He loves us. That is the simple truth. He chose to give up His life because of love. All He asks in return is that we believe. To me, that is easy. What about you?*

❏ Play the song "King of Glory" by Third Day or "Secret Ambition," by Michael W. Smith.

❏ After the song has played, read Acts 4:12 aloud. Plan a time of worship to follow. If possible, have someone lead in praise songs on the guitar. If a guitarist is not available, choose several songs from worship CDs to play during this time. Direct the youths' attention to the Jesus banner at the front of your meeting area. Explain to the youth that during this time of worship, you would like them to come and decorate the banner however they wish. They can write a prayer, draw a picture, write a praise, etc. Tell them that this activity is an act of worship. Encourage the youth to be creative and use the whole space as they work. Also explain that if anyone would like to talk further about accepting Christ as his personal Lord and Savior, someone will be available to talk during this time.

Close the Session

❏ Hang the banner at the front of the meeting area. Gather the students around and lead in prayer.

❏ Ask the students to keep their eyes open as you pray. Ask them to reflect on the banner and how each person displayed their worship during this time.

Learning Activity
Invitation to the Feast

Before the Session

❏ Find several adult volunteers to prepare ethnic dishes that will be served during the meal.

❏ Purchase the needed ingredients for the number of students who are expected to participate in the meal.

❏ Find two white flat sheets to represent tables. Lay them out on the floor of the area where you will be eating.

❏ Gather trays and serving utensils for three main dishes and several side dishes.

❏ Purchase cups and paper plates for the meal. Place one of each around the table for each participant.

❏ Locate a CD player and a CD of ethnic music to be played during the meal.

❏ Print and send an invitation to each of your students several weeks before the meal.

During the Session

❏ As students arrive, explain to them that they will be taking part in an ethnic feast. Play up the fact that each person that has arrived chose to accept the invitation you extended. Tell students that because it is an ethnic feast, they will have to follow some specific rules. Missionaries who are called to go to another country are usually faced with learning a new culture and new customs. Explain that you will be following the customs of the people of various other countries.

1. Everyone must remove their shoes and place them by the door.

2. Everyone must wash their hands before eating. This symbolizes a ritual of cleanliness.

3. Everyone will sit on the floor around the sheets. Women at one table, men at the other.

4. Everyone will eat using only their right hand.

5. Women will serve the men first and then sit to eat what is left.

❏ Ask students to remove their shoes and take their places at one of the tables. Provide a pitcher of water and a bowl to wash the students' hands. Have students place their hands together over the bowl. Have an adult volunteer pour water over their hands. No towels are provided for drying the hands. If you have a large group, have a pitcher and basin for each table.

❏ Begin the meal by saying a prayer of the Kouya people of Cote d'Ivoire. Ask the youth to repeat each line after you.

Lord God, Owner of earth and sky, we thank You.

You put Your good hand upon us, and You added this day to our years, and for this reason we give You thanks.

You have given us faith, and You have given us this food. For this we thank You.

Father God, put Your good hand on this food and bless it. Take out anything bad which may be in it, and when we've eaten, may we have peace.

In Your name and in Your Son, Jesus', name.

So be it.

(www.wycliff.org/catalog/Brightideas/home.htm, 2004)

❏ Have the women come and get the appetizer trays of tomatoes, nuts, and fruits. Women will take the trays back to serve the men. After the men have been served, the women will come back to their seats at the table and eat what has been left.

❏ As the appetizers are almost finished, stand up and tell the group that you will be reading them a story throughout the evening. Begin by reading Matthew 22:1–10. Relate the story to the feast you are participating in. Tell them that you would like to thank them for accepting your invitation to the feast. Ask: *What did you do in preparation for the feast?*

Did you dress differently than you normally would? Did you eat less for lunch in anticipation of the feast to come? Did you talk amongst yourselves about what was in store for you at the feast?

❏ Ask the women to come and get the main course. Have the women serve the men and then return to their table to eat what is left over.

❏ After the main course is finished, read Matthew 22:11–14. Ask for the reaction of the students to the ending of the story. Ask for their interpretation of the story. Ask: *What was Jesus trying to tell the people?*

Explain: *Just as in the story, we are all invited to the feast. Some will chose to come and some will ignore the invitation. This is evident in our world today. We can easily see how many people choose to ignore the invitation to accept Christ into their lives and there are even some who will laugh and mistreat those who invite them to come. And then there are those who will accept the invitation, but won't come prepared for the feast. They only come to be entertained or fed. They don't do anything to prepare their own hearts to accept the feast.*

Ask: *When you received your invitation, what did you think about the line that asked you to come appropriately prepared for the feast? Did you ask anyone what they thought that meant or did you just ignore it? Tonight we have experienced a feast. Now, I want you to think about why you chose to accept the invitation. Is your relationship with God where it needs to be? Have you accepted Christ into your heart? Are you worthy of being at the feast?*

❏ Present the ABCs of salvation to the group:
A—Admit, read Romans 3:23 and 6:23.
B—Believe, read John 20:31.
C—Confess, read Romans 10:9.
Take a few minutes to share your testimony about how you accepted Christ into your life. You can also invite a student or an adult volunteer to share a testimony at this time. Try to incorporate the theme of being invited to a feast into the testimony share time.

Close the Session

- Say: *In a moment we are going to share a dessert together. But this time, we are going to serve each other.*
- Have everyone sit in a circle with their heads bowed. Play some soft instrumental music in the background. Tell the students you will begin by choosing one person whom you will serve. You will get the dessert and place it in front of one student. After you have done this, you will then place your hands on this student's shoulders and say a prayer for that person. After the student has been prayed for, he will then get up and serve someone else. If a student is not comfortable praying aloud for another, instruct her that she can say a silent prayer and end with the word *amen* which will signal the next person to proceed. Tell students to be observant of who has a dessert in front of them. They must choose to serve someone who hasn't been served already.
- Once everyone has been served, the leader will close with a group prayer and everyone will enjoy dessert.

Ministry/Witnessing
Survivor: The Neighborhood

Before the Session

- Contact a local after-school program or Boys/Girls club to ask for permission to host an event. Make sure the program directors know you will be sharing Bible-related material with the children.
- Set a time and date to hold the activity.
- Secure adult volunteers, as well as an appropriate number of youth to host the event.
- Obtain two different colored twin flat sheets. Cut the sheets into strips so that each child will have a strip.
- Obtain two pieces of white poster board.
- Gather paint, brushes, and markers to be used for the event.
- If necessary, advertise the event in the neighborhood where you will be hosting the event.

- Choose a Bible verse that accompanies the Bible story you will be telling. Write each word of the verse on a separate index card. Write the verse twice, one for each team.
- Ask a youth volunteer to be prepared to share his/or her testimony during the event.
- Write out the following Scripture passages from a modern translation on separate sheets of poster board. Post the posters on trees along a path or road to resemble the "Roman Road."
  Romans 3:23
  Romans 6:23
  Romans 5:8
  Romans 6:12
  Romans 6:3–5

During the Session
Survivor: Coming to a Neighborhood Near You

- This activity is intended for a project through which students can minister to a group of children in grades 1–6.
- As children arrive for the event, divide them into two teams by giving them a colored strip of sheet. Children will be encouraged to wear the strip as a headband or armband throughout the event. Provide fabric markers for the children to write their names on the strips.
- When enough children have arrived, gather both teams together and welcome them to *Survivor: The Neighborhood!* Introduce who you are and why your group is there. Explain that for this event, the children will be playing a game that is similar to the TV show *Survivor.* Tell them there will be two challenges they will be participating in during the day. Explain that although the event is similar to the TV show, no one will be kicked out of the neighborhood!
- Begin by giving each team a piece of poster board or banner paper. Ask them to come up with a name for their team and to make a flag to represent the team. Provide paint and markers to make the flags.
- After 15 minutes, call both teams back together. Have them each bring their flags. Post the flags on the wall. Explain that the first challenge is about to take place. Have your youth group present a Bible story to the teams. This can be done by acting out the story. Choose a story that has a lot of action in it,

like Noah's Ark or Jonah and the big fish. After the story presentation is over, tell the children that each team will have to answer some specific questions about the story they just heard. Have each team line up as if they are going to run a relay race. Place two youth at one end of the room and the children at the opposite end behind a designated line. Tell the children they will take turns running to the youth who will ask them a question about the story. The child will have to answer the question correctly for the youth. If the child gets the answer correct, they will be given one word of a Bible verse. They will take that word back to the team and lay it on the ground. If the person gets the answer wrong, they must return to the team with nothing. The game will continue until the teams get all the words of the Bible verse. Once they have all the words, they must work together to put the verse in order. The team that puts the verse in order first will win the challenge.

❏ After the first challenge, take a break and have drinks and snacks available. Keep the survivor theme going by providing water, bananas, gummy worms, popcorn, etc. Be creative! During this time, have a youth share his or her testimony. If possible, have her relate the testimony to the game of survivor. After the testimony time, have the youth share the plan of salvation by sharing the Scriptures of the Roman Road. This can be done by reading and explaining the Scriptures or through acting out skits for each Scripture verse. Allow the youth to be creative in how they will present the Scripture.

❏ The second challenge will come after the break. This challenge will focus on telling the story of salvation through the Roman Road. Place the five posters that have the Roman Road Scriptures written on them along a path or in five different rooms of the building where you are holding the event. Tell the children that at each station they will have to perform a stunt. If the stunt is performed correctly, they will be given a Bible verse to write down. Once they have completed all five stunts they will have five Bible verses. They will need to put the Bible verses in order according to what they have been taught earlier. The first team with them in the correct order will win.

Stunts:

Romans 3:23—Each person has to chew a piece of gum and blow a bubble.

Romans 6:23—The team must make a pyramid. This can be a flat pyramid where students are lying down or a standing pyramid.

Romans 5:8—The team must spell out *survivor* with their bodies, one letter at a time.

Romans 6:12—The team must dig through a container of sand and find all the letters that spell *Survivor: The Neighborhood*. They must put them in order to spell the phrase.

Romans 6:3–5—The team must form a single file line and pass a wet sponge over, under, over, under down the line to fill a cup with water. If they don't fill it the first time, the last person must run to the front of the line, dunk the sponge in the bucket again and repeat the process until the cup has been filled.

Close the Session

❏ Have a youth share a testimony about her life with Christ. Tell the children that if any of them are interested in knowing more about what it means to have a personal relationship with Christ, they can talk to any of the youth or adults who are present. Close the time with prayer for the children who attended.

❏ Give each child some type of prize to take home with them to remember the day and to invite them to the next event that you will be hosting and to your church.

Cultural Experience
Reaching International Students

Before the Session

❏ Identify international students who live in your area. If you don't have a college nearby, contact your Baptist state convention for help.

❏ Collect a shoe box for each student who you will minister to through the project.

❏ Send out a flyer to each of your students and their families regarding the details of the project. Ask for donations from the church for the following items:

- laundry bags
- laundry detergent (tablets or small containers)
- stain stick
- dryer sheets
- quarters
- snack items (crackers, chips, candy bars, gum, etc.)
- magazines (for men and women)

❑ Gather supplies for making cards and wrapping the boxes: construction paper, stickers, markers, glue, crayons, plain wrapping paper, etc.

During the Session

This ministry project will focus on international college students. If you do not have a college in your town, contact your state Baptist convention for contact information of a college Baptist student ministry in your state that has a ministry to international students.

❑ Contact the Baptist student ministry at the college. Tell the director that your group would like to collect laundry supplies for international students on campus. Ask for their help with the distribution process.

❑ Designate a time to put the collected supplies into the boxes. Make sure that each box contains the same items. Boxes should be covered and decorated by the youth. Use patriotic colors and the greeting *Welcome to (your state or city)* on the front. If you choose to include a magazine in the box, make sure that there is a distinction between the men's and the women's boxes.

❑ Include a prayer card in each box. Ask the youth to make a card that will be put in the box. Have them write a prayer for the student who will receive the box. Include your church information on the card, if it is appropriate to do so, and information about the Baptist student ministry.

Close the Session

❑ If the college is in your town, set a time when your group can deliver the boxes personally. If not, mail the packages to the Baptist student ministry that will be distributing the boxes.

Missionary Ministry
Josh and Amy Bowman (Luwingu, Zambia)

Before the Session

❑ Write the prayer requests listed under After the Session on individual pieces of construction paper. Hang the posters around the room or down a long corridor to simulate a prayerwalk experience.

❑ Read through the story about Josh and Amy Bowman (p. 15). Be prepared to tell their story in your own words.

❑ Check out the Web site: www.bmoz.org to find out up-to-date information about the Bowmans and the work that is going on in Zambia with the Bemba people group.

During the Session

❑ As students arrive, divide them into five different groups. Assign each group one of the following Bible stories: creation, David and Goliath, birth of Jesus, Jesus feeds the 5,000, and Jesus' death and resurrection. Ask students to imagine that they are missionaries to Zambia, Africa. Tell them that the people group they will work with does not know how to read their own language. You will have to tell them stories from the Bible in order for them to understand the message of salvation. Have each group read their Bible story and figure out a way to present that story verbally. Each student must take part in the telling of the story. Give groups 15 minutes to work on their presentation. Have groups tell their stories to the large group.

❑ When groups have finished telling their stories, tell them about missionaries Josh and Amy Bowman.

❑ Ask: *Would it be hard for you to leave your home and family to go and do what Josh and Amy have been called to do? Why or why not?*

What would be scary/exciting about going to another country to live and serve Christ as a missionary?

Was it easy to tell your Bible story? Can you think of other ways to share the gospel message without reading it out of the Bible?

Close the Session

❏ Create a prayerwalk for Zambia. Have each student find a partner for this activity. Post the prayer requests around the room or down a long hallway. Establish a pattern that students will follow and ask them to visit each sign and pray for Josh and Amy Bowman's requests.

Prayer Requests for Josh and Amy Bowman

• Pray for Josh, Amy, Caleb, and Abigail Bowman. Pray that they will remain healthy and strong to continue their work with the Bembas.

• Pray for Josh and his ministry through storytelling. Pray that the people he teaches are receptive to the gospel story.

• Pray for Amy as she balances family responsibilities and discipling women in the village.

• Pray for Caleb and Abigail as they grow up in Zambia. Ask for God's protection over them.

• Pray for both Josh and Amy as they continue to learn the Chibemba language. May their words be clear to the people and may they be able to understand their questions with ease.

• Pray that God would move mightily through the villages of the Bemba people. May they come to know Jesus as their Lord and Savior.

• Pray for the Bowmans' family who lives here in the US. Pray that they would be supportive of their children and their calling to share the gospel overseas.

Josh and Amy Bowman

Josh and Amy Bowman are missionaries from Jacksonville, Florida, who serve in Luwingu, Zambia. After high school, Josh and Amy had an opportunity to go on an overseas missions trip to the Philippines. It was on that trip that they both felt called to the missions field. Josh and Amy were later married and continued to feel God's calling to the harvest field where people would be receptive and responsive to the gospel. God lead them to Africa and the town of Luwingu. This small town is located about 12 hours away from the capital city, Lusaka. It is so small that there are no grocery stores, gas stations, or paved roads! The Bowmans work with a people group called the Bemba [bim-BAH]

Josh teaches the Bemba people about Jesus through Bible storying. His job is to tell stories from the Bible chronologically, starting with creation and leading up to salvation. Josh visits nearby villages and talks to their traditional leaders, known as "headmen." After explaining what he wants to teach, they set up a time when he will come back to share his stories and teach them about the Bible and Jesus

Amy works as a stay-at-home mom with their two children, Caleb and Abigail. She also serves as a discipler for women from the villages who want to know more about Jesus

The Bemba people are very poor and many suffer from AIDS, a disease that is spread through sexual promiscuity and blood transfusions. The people survive by farming on plots of bush. They produce crops of finger millet (a type of grain) and cassava (a vegetable that is similar to a sweet potato).

The King's Son

There once was great king who ruled a vast kingdom. Now the king was very powerful and all of his subjects feared him greatly. They all knew that the king ruled fairly but severely punished disobedience. To go against the king meant certain death. The king had a son. Being the only son of the king he was also very rich and possessed everything he wanted. However despite all of his riches the son did lack one thing. You see, to be the son of the king meant that he had lots of servants but no one with whom to share his friendship, time, or possessions.

From time to time the king and his son would take a ride through the kingdom. They did this on their horses, and when they did they would take some of their mounted guards with them. On one of these trips as they rode near a village, the son noticed a group of young people playing in a field. The son immediately wished he could join them, but as they approached, the group of youth stopped their games, quietly bowed to the king and then turned and ran away. At this, the son's face dropped with disappointment and his father, the king, noticed it. When they got home, the king went to his son and asked what was troubling him. The son replied "I am rich and blessed, yet I wish I had some friends to share it with. Friends I could be close to, spend time with, and love, but everyone seems to be afraid of me."

The king then asked, "How important is this to you?"

"Very," said the son, "I often think I would give all I have just to have friends."

At this the king thought a moment. Then he said, "Come with me." He led the son down to the stable where the servants kept the horses. Here he spoke for a minute to the head stable keeper and then turned to the son.

"Son," he said, "as long as you are known to our subjects as the king's son, they will do everything you ask. If you ask to play in one of their games they will agree, if you ask one to come have dinner with you he will accept, but all this will be for one reason, because you are the son of the king and because they fear my power. If you wish them to be your friends because they want to, you must become as one of them. Are you willing to do this for friendship?"

The son thought for a minute and then with a joyful grin said, "Yes!" The king then instructed the son.

"First take off your rich clothing and put on the clothes of the stable boys."

The son did so and said, "OK, I'm ready now—let's go," but the king did not move.

Instead he said, "For the next three years you will work here in the stable. Here you will not only start to look like them, but also to act like them." And with that the king left.

The son was shocked, "Three years here first!" he said. Yet despite his disappointment he set to work executing the chores given him by the stable master. During the next three years the son worked hard. His hands grew calloused and he learned what it was like to be tired and dirty and hungry. And each day while he worked he longed for the day to come when he could go and join those subjects who would become his friends.

After three years the king returned and took him from the stable. He gave him a new set of clothes that looked much like those the poorest of his subjects wore and took him to a field a great distance from the palace. There he sent him off on his journey to find friendship. As he said good-bye, he gave the son one final instruction. "When you have made friends and wish to return, come back to this field and light a signal fire here and I will return for you." Then the king left.

Once alone, the son set out walking and by nightfall he found a village. There he found a place to stay. Since he had no money he slept in the barn with the animals. The next day, he found some young men working in a field and asked if he could join them. They agreed and he began to work alongside of them. Over the next three years the son worked and lived in this village and just as he had hoped, he made friends, many friends. He worked with them, he played with them, and he cried with them, and as he did he became close to many.

The time came for his birthday and he decided to have a party with his new friends. *My party,* he thought, *will be a special day.* At his party, he would announce to all his friends who he was and take them back to the palace for the best party he could imagine.

The next day the son ran all day back to the field where he had started his journey and there lit the signal fire his father had instructed him three years before. As he lay in bed that night he thought, *At last, I have made many friends. I have found love and friendship all offered freely for me. I am so excited, for now I can tell them who I am and take them out of this poverty.* As the son fell asleep that night he was full of joy.

The next day, the son called all his friends together for the announcement. Over a hundred of them were in the village courtyard having a great time when suddenly a great mounted party of riders arrived. It was the procession of the king. All the son's friends suddenly became very quiet. Some of them quietly left, others pulled back from the procession and hid themselves in the buildings. Others watched in fear as the horses and riders of the king's guard filled the courtyard. As they watched, the king dismounted and walked up to their friend. The king embraced their friend and spoke something to him. What was happening they thought?

Then the son got up and stood on the backs of two of the horses. All fell silent as he spoke. The son said, "My friends, I am the son of the king, the prince." He went on to let all his friends know that they had been chosen to go with him and live as his guests in the palace of the king. Yet as he spoke, he noticed the faces of his friends were full of fear. Many were quietly slipping away. He turned to look at his closest friends and even their faces had turned white and they were backing away from him.

Seeing this he turned to his father and cried, "Why is this? Father, Why do they still fear us?" The king motioned to the captain of his guard and the captain came forward and held out an open book to the son. The son took it and began to read.

The book held a list of names and as he read them he recognized them as the names of each of his friends. Beside each name was a crime against the king, and beside each crime there was a date. Beside each date was a sentence. In every case, the sentence was death. As the son read name after name, crime after crime, tears came to his eyes. Now the awful truth became clear. These people fear us because they know they have broken the king's laws and now that we are here, they are under the sentence of death. The son was filled with grief.

The son now turned quietly to the father. "Father," he said, "I have found great joy in the friendship of these. Is there any way they can be spared?"

The father saw the son's grief and his own heart was torn. "My son, we cannot break our own laws for they are our word. The penalty for disobedience must be paid. The only way they can be spared is for someone to pay the penalty for them. But since everyone of them has broken the law there is no one who can take another's place."

The son thought for a moment and then asked, "Father, can I take their sentences?"

"Yes," the father said, "but not for all, only for those who believe that what you do is for them."

With that, the son once again mounted the two horses, and in a loud voice he said, "My friends, you are all under the penalty of death, yet I love you and my father has given me permission to take your sentence so that you might live." When he was finished, at the king's instruction, the captain of the guard took the son, bound him and there in the middle of the courtyard put him to death. The king did not speak again, but quietly watched his son die. The king's guard then took the son's body and placed it on a horse and the king's procession left the courtyard.

Now the friends of the son were in shock at what they had seen. They spent many days trying to understand the last words he had said. No one ever saw the king out riding again and in time, most of the friends forgot what had happened. But a few of the son's closest friends never forgot the sacrifice this friend had made for them.

Source:
www.psiaz.com/backdoorbible/html/kingson.htm

Recipes

CHICKEN TANDOORI

1 4-pound chicken (whole, portions, or drumsticks)

2 medium onions

1 teaspoon chili powder

½ cup plain yogurt

1 tablespoon vinegar

4 cloves garlic

1 tablespoon Worcestershire sauce

2 tablespoons ginger root

1 teaspoon garam masala (a spice from Asian or Indian grocery stores)

1 teaspoon ground coriander

2 tablespoons butter

1 teaspoon ground cumin

4 tablespoons lemon juice

salt to taste

1. Wash the chicken. Make 3 or 4 cuts on each side of the bird or on each portion so seasonings can seep into meat.

2. Grind onion, garlic, and ginger to a paste and then add the cumin, coriander, chili, garam masala, and salt.

3. Beat the yogurt in a bowl. Add the paste from step 2, vinegar, Worcestershire sauce, and half the lemon juice. Mix thoroughly.

4. Rub the mixture on the chicken and allow it to marinate for 5 hours.

5. Preheat the oven to 375ºF. Roast chicken in pan for 1½ hours or until thoroughly cooked. Baste with remaining lemon juice and butter every 30 minutes. Cut into portions and serve.

AFRICAN GROUNDNUT STEW

3 pounds pork or chicken

4 tablespoons tomato puree

3 medium onions

6 cups chicken stock

1 red pepper

salt to taste

2 tablespoons oil

1 16-ounce jar of peanut butter, preferably no oil or sugar added

1. Cut meat into bite-sized chunks, stir fry and set aside. (Leave out meat for vegetarian version over rice.) Meat is an expensive treat.

2. Chop and fry onions in oil.

3. Stir in peanut butter and fry for two more minutes.

4. Add stock gradually to form a smooth sauce.

5. Mix tomato puree with a little water and add to the pan.

6. Add chopped red pepper and salt.

7. Add meat and serve.

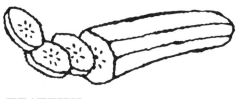

TZATZIKI

½ quart Greek yogurt (or natural full, dairy yogurt)

3 garlic cloves

½ cup olive oil

½ peeled, thin-sliced cucumber

1. Put the yogurt in a bowl. Put the garlic through a garlic press and, using the edge of a knife, spread the garlic coming out of the press on the yogurt.

2. Take the cucumber and peel the skin. Slice it thinly, and put it into the yogurt.

3. Mix the ingredients with a mixer (or a fork) and slowly add the oil. The oil will be absorbed, and when it is, the tzatziki is ready.

4. Serve with a spoon and a few olives spread on the top.

Tzatziki is eaten with plenty of French bread.

TOMATO CHUTNEY

1 pound tomatoes
2 cloves garlic
½ cup sugar
¼ cup raisins
½ cup malt vinegar
1 teaspoon chili powder
1 teaspoon ginger powder
salt to taste

1. Peel tomatoes and cut into quarters.
2. Finely chop garlic.
3. Simmer tomatoes, ginger, garlic, chili, and salt until the tomatoes are pulpy.
4. Add sugar, vinegar, raisins, and cook until the mixture thickens.
5. Allow to cool. Serve, or refrigerate and use at later date.

YELLOW RICE

3 cups white rice
2 teaspoons ground turmeric
6 cups water
2 teaspoons salt, or salt to taste

1. Whisk the turmeric and water together.
2. Bring water to a boil and add the salt. Pour in rice and stir until the water returns to a boil. (With instant rice, simply follow package directions, but add the turmeric and salt to water first.)
3. Cover with lid and simmer for twenty minutes or until the rice is tender and water is absorbed. With other types of rice, simply cook according to package directions. Brown rice takes longer and requires more water, for instance.
4. Serve hot.

Pita bread or flat tortilla-like breads can be used to scoop the food off the plates to eat. The bread can be torn into small squares and placed between the thumb and first two fingers as a scoop. Youth can pinch up some food and quickly scoop it into their mouths.

For drinking, water should be dipped out of a clean bucket into cups.

INDIAN DAHL

1½ pounds red lentils
2 tablespoons butter or oil
2 medium onions finely sliced
3 cloves garlic
1 tablespoon ginger root
1 teaspoon ground turmeric
1 teaspoon ground cumin
1½ cups hot water
1 teaspoon salt
1 teaspoon garam masala
(a spice from Asian or Indian grocery stores)

1. Wash lentils thoroughly and remove those that float to surface.
2. Finely chop onion, garlic, and ginger.
3. Heat oil and fry onion, garlic, and ginger until onion is golden.
4. Add turmeric and cumin. Stir well.
5. Add drained lentils and stir for two minutes on medium high heat.
6. Add hot water, bring to boil and simmer on low heat, covered, for about 15 minutes until lentils are about half cooked.
7. Add salt and garam masala. Mix well and continue to cook until lentils are soft and of the consistency of porridge or thick oatmeal.
8. If there's too much liquid, leave lid off pan and simmer longer.

Sources: Tzatziki from www.elikioliveoil.com/ tzatziki.html. All others from www.wycliff.org/ catalog/Brightideas/home.htm

Unit 3
Growing in Christ

Introduction
Do You Need to Be Pruned?

I have always wanted to be described as a person who has a green thumb. My husband has one. I think he could make a stick sprout in stale water! Something about the growing process eludes me. My idea of taking care of plants is to water them and stick them on a window sill. If they don't grow, I give up. That is why my husband is in charge of the plants in our house. He takes time to water them and removes the dead leaves. He handles them gently and turns them when they need sunlight from another angle. He repots them when they grow too large, and he watches over them when they look sick.

One of our most prized plants is an orchid. When it is in bloom, it has the most beautiful, radiant, purple flowers. Everyone who visits our home comments on its beauty. Recently, my husband decided the orchid needed to be repotted. We bought a pot and he went to work. When he took the orchid out of its old pot, it was obvious it needed a new home. The roots were tightly wound around each other. There was no room for it to grow. Steve began by gently shaking the dirt away from the roots to loosen them from their bondage, but the roots would not let go. They had been in that position so long that they had taken on the shape of the pot. Steve then began to cut the roots. He cut so much that I predicted the plant's demise. Yet, to my amazement, the orchid survived and is now putting out more beautiful blooms than ever!

Like the orchid, there are times when we become root-bound and must be challenged to grow in a new environment.

It is so easy for us to become comfortable with things as they are. We don't want to be challenged to do more, study more, or even share God's Word with those we come in contact with in our daily lives. There comes a time when God says, "It is time for you to grow," and He begins to cut our roots back.

This unit will challenge youth to evaluate their relationship with Christ. They will identify areas in their lives where they need to be more like Christ. They will also be challenged to find new ways to grow.

Bible Study
Christian Growth

Before the Session

❏ Ask each student to bring a baby picture of him- or herself to the next meeting. Stress to students that they should not show their pictures to others in the session. Prepare a bulletin board or poster board where the youth can display their pictures as they arrive. Number each picture. Include pictures of yourself and other adult leaders in the church.

❏ Prepare seven paper bags with the following words written boldly on each one: *goodness, knowledge, self-control, perseverance, godliness, brotherly kindness, love*. Fill each bag with three random items. The items can be anything, but no three things should be related. Example: a spoon, spool of thread, and a dog collar.

❏ You will need a chalkboard or marker board and copies of "Guess Who" worksheet (p. 23).

❏ Be familiar with Scripture verses that will be emphasized during the lesson.

During the Session

❏ As the youth arrive, have them give you their baby pictures. Keep the identity of each picture a secret. Display the pictures on the bulletin board that you prepared. Make sure that each of the pictures has a number displayed underneath it.

❏ After the majority of the group has arrived, have them fill out the "Guess Who?" worksheet. After ten minutes, reveal the identity of each picture.

❏ Use this activity as a time to discuss the importance of growth. We start out as babies and continue to grow throughout our lives. We grow in size, height, and mind. Explain that God's intent is that we also grow in our relationship with Him. Have a volunteer read Ephesians 4:15–16. Ask someone in the group to explain the verse in his or her own words.

❏ Ask: *What can we do in order to grow in our relationship with Christ?*

❏ Write the responses on a chalkboard or marker board. Ask another volunteer to read 2 Peter 1:5–9. Have students list the seven qualities of a basic faith on the board.

❏ Divide the students into groups of two. Give each group a grocery bag full of random items. Using the items that are in the bag, each group must come up with a skit that will depict the word that is written on the front of the bag. Allow the groups ten minutes to come up with their skits. Have each group perform their skit. After each skit, discuss the meaning of the word that the skit was based on. Ask students to explain why they think that characteristic is important to our Christian growth.

Close the Session

❏ Have students get back in their groups and share one characteristic that they need to work on during the next month.

❏ Have the groups pray together and commit to be accountable to each other throughout the month.

❏ Encourage the students to call their partner during the week and hold them accountable to their commitment.

Learning Activity
More Like Christ

Before the Session

❏ Collect various celebrity magazines and newspapers. Set up a table where the students can work when they arrive. Put glue sticks, scissors, markers, and colored paper in the middle of the table.

❏ Purchase small sticky notes.

❏ Construct a cross on the wall out of brown construction paper.

❏ Have a CD player available for use During the Session.

❏ Purchase the song "Clumsy" by Chris Rice (*Past the Edges* CD).

❏ Purchase leather strips and cut to an appropriate length to be tied around a student's wrist.

During the Session

❏ As youth arrive, direct them to the tables where you have set up the magazines. Instruct them to look through the magazines and cut out pictures to make a montage of the attributes that would make up the "perfect" person. Help the students to not only focus on the appearance of the individual, but also, the personality traits of the individual.

❏ After ten minutes, have the students sit in a circle with their montages. Ask for several volunteers to share their pictures with the group. After several have shared, ask the following questions:

  • *Would your montage look different if I had asked you to create a picture of the perfect Christian? If so, how?*

  • *Do you know anyone who comes close to being the perfect Christian?*

  • *What does that person do that makes others think that of them?*

❏ Read Philippians 2:5–11.

❏ Lead in a discussion about how Christ was perfect in every way and we are to strive to be like Christ. Even though perfection is not attainable, it is our job to strive for perfection in our own lives.

Guess Who?

Do you think you know your youth group? Well, now is your chance to show it! Look at each of the baby pictures on the display. Beside the number that corresponds to each picture, name the youth in the picture. Be careful . . . you may be surprised along the way!

1._____

2._____

3._____

4._____

5._____

6._____

7._____

8._____

9._____

10._____

11._____

12._____

13._____

14._____

15._____

Guess Who?

Do you think you know your youth group? Well, now is your chance to show it! Look at each of the baby pictures on the display. Beside the number that corresponds to each picture, name the youth in the picture. Be careful . . . you may be surprised along the way!

1._____

2._____

3._____

4._____

5._____

6._____

7._____

8._____

9._____

10._____

11._____

12._____

13._____

14._____

15._____

❏ Give each student several sticky notes. Ask the students to find a place in the room where they can be alone and reflect on the song that you will play. As the song plays, have the students write down several things in their own lives that they need to work on as they strive to be more like Christ. Encourage them to write only one word per note. Have the students stick the note to the cross as a reminder that they will strive to be more like Christ in their daily walk.

Close the Session

❏ Give each student a piece of leather to wear as a bracelet. As students wear the leather bands throughout the week, tell them that the bands are to serve as reminders to be more like Christ when the youth are at school, at work, with friends, or at home.

Ministry/Witnessing
Mentoring Program

Before the Session

❏ Contact your local neighborhood or community center and ask if your youth group can develop a mentoring program with the children who participate in the center's programs.

❏ Make sure that the community center director is aware that your group is a Christian group of young people. Get permission to share the gospel message in the activities you plan.

❏ Make one copy of the "Bible Hunt" for each group of five (p. 25).

❏ Purchase prizes to be awarded.

During the Session

❏ This activity will be a great way to establish a relationship between each youth and three or four of the children who are participating in the mentoring program.

❏ Divide the group into an equal number of smaller groups. Assign one youth to a group of three or four children. If possible, keep boys and girls separate.

❏ Give each group a copy of the "Bible Hunt" sheet. Explain that the groups are going to go on a special scavenger hunt. On the handout, they will see a list of Bible characters. The object will be for each team to find an item that relates to the story of that character. For example, if the name is David, an object that would be appropriate would be a stone or a slingshot. Either item would be acceptable. The only stipulation is items cannot be taken or borrowed without permission.

❏ Each group will have one hour to find as many objects as possible. Give each group a Bible and let them go! (Adapted from www.ega-dideas.com.)

Close the Session

❏ When all the teams return, tally up the items and award a prize to the team that brought back the most items.

❏ End the event with a time of fellowship. Provide refreshments and allow the groups to tell stories of their adventures.

Cultural Experience
Fiesta

Before the Session

❏ Enlist volunteers to promote the fiesta and to get an accurate count of people to attend.

❏ Enlist a team to decorate. Simple decorations can be red and green crepe paper streamers rolled down the middle of white tablecloths. Place mixed dried beans in clear glass bowls to hold red or green candles. Add ears of dried corn for a colorful Christmas fiesta. To decorate for a Mexican Christmas, be sure to add some beautiful red poinsettias or "La Flor De Noche Buena." Poinsettias have been a Christmas tradition throughout much of the world since an American ambassador introduced the plant to South Carolina in the 1820s.

❏ Enlist a team to plan, purchase, and prepare the food. Make sure enough adults are on this team. Possible menu items include: chips and salsa or cheese dip or guacamole; a make-your-own taco or fajita bar with chicken or hamburger, shredded lettuce, salsa or finely

Bible Scavenger Hunt

The object of this scavenger hunt is to find items that relate to the Bible stories of the following people. For example, for the name David, you can find a stone or a slingshot to represent the story of David and Goliath. Beside each name, write the item your group has selected, as well as the story the item comes from in the Bible.

Noah _____

Moses _____

Adam _____

David _____

Zaccheus _____

Mary, the mother of Jesus _____

Peter _____

Jonah _____

Ruth _____

Esther _____

Daniel _____

John _____

Jesus _____

Martha _____

Lazarus _____

chopped tomatoes, shredded cheese; beans; rice; cookies or flan for dessert (some stores carry flan mixes in the pudding area).

❑ Enlist volunteers to plan activities and entertainment. Possibilities include: a speaker who has volunteered as a short-term missionary in Mexico, a Mexican-American to tell about his or her own Christmas memories in Mexico and traditions they still keep in the United States, or someone who has vacationed in Mexico; someone who can teach some Christmas carols in Spanish or sing a solo; or simply a CD playing Mexican-style music. Part of this teams' responsibilities also includes greeting people, providing name tags, and enlisting an emcee for the evening and someone to offer a blessing for the food. For an ice breaker, cut out small sombreros—enough for all participants—with an equal number of each of these words: sombrero, fiesta, poinsettia, peso, mariachi, tamale. Tape one to each person's back. Students will ask questions to discover their word. Everyone with the same word will eat at the same table and play on the same team for any subsequent games. Games may include relays using sombreros, making the most words out of Feliz Navidad, or using red, green, and white crepe paper streamers to "wrap" one of their team members to become the most attractive present.

OPTION: An option for this session is to have the party at a Mexican restaurant. Adapt the activities according to the space available. Ask in advance for a private room and for waiters who will chat with students about their culture and Christmas in Mexico. If the owners or managers of the restaurant are Christians, you may want to ask one to tell about being a Christian in Mexico. Encourage students to use a few Spanish words in talking with the waiters.

During the Session

❑ Welcome guests with appropriate greetings in Spanish.
❑ Play ice breaker.
❑ Offer blessing for food.
❑ Go through buffet line and enjoy the feast!
❑ Listen to speakers or entertainers.

❑ Play games.
❑ Read the Christmas story in Spanish.
❑ Close by singing a carol in Spanish or "Silent Night" in English.

Close the Session

❑ Everyone stays to help clean and to leave everything in even better shape than it was originally.

Missionary Ministry
Lloyd and Connie Rodgers (Colombia)

Before the Session

❑ Plan to hold this session at a local coffee shop. If there is not one available in your area, plan to hold the meeting in someone's home. Serve Colombian coffee to the students.
❑ Prepare a recipe of Patacones (Fried Plantains) to be served during the meeting (p. 26).
❑ Gather Bibles and concordances that will be available for research.
❑ Familiarize yourself with the story of missionaries Lloyd and Connie Rodgers (p. 28). Be ready to tell the story in your own words.

During the Session

❑ Begin the session by serving students a cup of Colombian coffee. Serve fried plantains as a treat.

PATACONES
(FRIED PLANTAINS)

4 large green plantains
vegetable oil
salt

Peel the plantains and cut into 3–4 pieces. Fry in hot vegetable oil. When plantains are golden, take them out of the oil and pound them flat. Return them to the oil and refry for a few minutes. Remove and place on absorbent paper. Sprinkle salt to taste.

- Share the story of Lloyd and Connie Rodgers.
- After sharing the story, divide the students into three small groups. Explain that one of the Rodgers' jobs is to find ways to reach professionals and students with the gospel message. Assign each group one of the following scenarios the Rodgers have dealt with in their ministry. Ask students to read the scenario and decide how they would respond in the situation.
- Have each group share their scenario and what they would do in that particular situation.

Close the Session

- Share the prayer requests below with the students. Have students return to their groups and assign each group one of the prayer requests. Have each group spend a few minutes in prayer for the Rodgers and their work.

Prayer Requests for Lloyd and Connie Rodgers

• Pray for the Rodgers and their two daughters, Anna and Katie. Pray for God's guidance and protection.

• Pray for the students who attend the seminary where Lloyd and Connie teach. Pray that they may they be able to reach their country for Christ.

• Pray for innovative ideas for reaching the professionals and students in the major cities of Colombia.

SCENARIOS

Scenario One

Maria is a typical professional in a major city of Colombia. She is the mother of two adult children, both of whom are recent university graduates. Maria's husband owns several fishing boats and has interests in the canning industry. Maria works as a volunteer coordinator for the five largest hospitals in the city. Maria has recently accepted Jesus into her life. She is currently the only Christian in her family.

Many professionals in Colombia have weekend homes. They leave the city on Friday afternoons and return on Sunday evenings. This presents a problem for the Rodgers as they invite people to traditional Sunday services. What would you do, if you were trying to reach the professionals and students of Colombia? Plan a worship service that would attract this population.

Scenario Two

It seems that God is moving among university students in Colombia. The Rodgers have seen a number of decisions for Christ on the university campuses. In particular, there is a soldier at the university who is heavily involved with a pagan, spiritualist religion. He is struggling with the concept of a loving Savior. What would you tell this student? Find some Scripture verses that would comfort him and reassure him of God's love.

Scenario Three

Christian and Norman are two university students with whom the Rodgers recently shared the gospel message. After talking for several hours, the students were still unsure about accepting Christ as their Savior. They wanted to know more about the resurrection of Jesus. In particular they wanted to know the proofs for the resurrection of Christ. What Scripture would you share with Christian and Norman? Make a good argument for the resurrection of Christ. Find Scripture verses that will support your argument.

Lloyd and Connie Rodgers

Barranquilla

Monteria

Cucuta

Medellin

Rio Magdalena

Bogota

Cali

COLOMBIA

Pasto

Mitu

Lloyd and Connie Rodgers are missionaries to Colombia. They work as teachers in theological education. (Point out the location of Colombia on a globe or map.)

The Rodgers felt called to serve during a Baptist Student Union retreat. The missionary speaker during the retreat was from the Philippines. He told of preaching to the communist guerillas in the mountains and traveling from village to village to share God's Word. The idea of identifying with different cultures and making the gospel culturally relevant was a concept that appealed to Lloyd. After graduation, he spent two years as a Journeyman in Singapore. It was during this experience that Lloyd knew God was calling him to serve on the missions field. The Rodgers' calling to Latin America was confirmed as they continued to hear of the need for theological educators who were dedicated to planting churches and to sharing their vision for Latin America with students.

The seminary where the Rodgers teach has about 100 students from Colombia as well as other South American countries. The School of Missions of the seminary was founded to train Colombians who respond to a missionary calling. Lloyd and Connie teach many different classes. These include missiology, church planting strategies, evangelism methods, urban missions, biblical basis for missions, history of missions, and chronological Bible storying.

In addition to their teaching, the Rodgers also plant churches among professional/career people and college students. They encounter all kinds of people who are hungry for the gospel message. Many people are responding to Jesus. This is evident in the growth of home Bible studies and the start of new churches.

Colombia is known around the world as a place of violence. It leads the world in kidnappings, homicides, and heroine production. An entire generation of Colombians have grown up listening to daily accounts of deaths and political threats. According to Lloyd, the statistics easily overshadow the reality of life. The Rodgers describe the city as "beautiful, peaceful, and civic-minded." The vast majority of people in the region are horrified of the violence and history of drugs. Lloyd states that their daily routine is fairly normal and they do not live in fear.

Unit 4
Deepening Your Relationship with God Through Worship

Introduction
Are You Prepared?

As 1999 ended and the year 2000 began, some people had a concern that problems would arise as the new century started. The media warned the public to be prepared for possible consequences associated with the century date change. Some "experts" predicted that at the strike of midnight, computers around the world would crash causing problems with all aspects of life as we know it.

The reaction of the public was varied. Some people immediately stockpiled food in their basements. They bought large drums of water, filled their freezers with meat and vegetables, and purchased multi-packs of paper towels and toilet paper! Others ignored the hoopla and decided if something happened they would go to their mother's house and live off her stockpile.

I recently met a man who had stockpiled. My husband and I were searching for a house to purchase. During one of our house visits, we found ourselves in the basement of the gentleman's home. He had collected an enormous amount of supplies in response to the Y2K scare. He had canned goods, barrels of water, toilet paper, paper towels, canned milk, and many other nonperishable items. So much stuff was stacked around the room; you could barely walk through it. As he showed us the room, he laughed and said, "It never hurts to be prepared!"

The following unit focuses on preparing our hearts, minds, and spirits for worship. So many times we come to God when we are tired, weary, or preoccupied. Worship becomes a time when we just go through the motions. We haven't taken the time to prepare; we assume that the pastor, worship leader, or Sunday school teacher will do the preparation for us.

Students will be challenged to evaluate what life obstacles are preventing them from experiencing true worship. They will discover what it means to be prepared to meet God in worship and learn what they need to do in order to be prepared in heart, mind, and spirit.

Bible Study
Be Prepared?

Before the Session

❑ Make a banner that will hang at the front of the meeting room with the caption *Be Prepared* written in bold letters.

❑ Write the following activities on individual index cards: *Going camping, Going on a date, Making Thanksgiving dinner, Planning a wedding.*

❑ Read and study Psalm 15 and John 4:24.

❑ Make sure there is a chalkboard, flip chart, or marker board available for use during the session.

❑ Ask someone to lead worship songs at the end of the session. If someone is not available to play the guitar or keyboard, prepare to play a worship CD with songs on it the students know.

During the Session

❑ As students enter the room, assign them to one of four groups. Give each group an index card that has been labeled according to the directions above. Explain that for the next month the group will be focusing on worship: what it is, why we do it, and the purpose of it. Have the students look at the banner at the front of the room and ask what the importance is of preparation. Allow several students to share their thoughts on why it is important to be prepared. Ask each group to read their index card and make a list of what they would need to do in order to be prepared for that particular situation. Allow students five minutes to brainstorm. Bring the groups back together and allow them time to share their ideas with the larger group. After each group has shared, ask the larger group to add any step they may have left out.

❏ After the activity, share with the group your thoughts on being prepared. Explain to them the importance of your preparation for the lesson. What would happen if you hadn't prepared? Would they notice? Explain that in worship we must come prepared. We must prepare our hearts, minds, and spirits for worship.

❏ Spend some time talking about how we should be prepared to meet God when we come to worship on Sunday or Wednesday evenings.

❏ Ask a volunteer to read Psalm 15 aloud. If possible, use a contemporary translation of the Bible like *The Message* during this time. Ask the group to identify the characteristics God lays out for one who comes prepared to worship. Write the characteristics on the chalkboard, flip chart, or marker board. Have another volunteer read John 4:24 aloud. Ask, *What does this verse tell us to do to be prepared for worship?*

❏ Ask the students to share their thoughts about the verses and how they relate to their lives on a daily basis. Lead in a discussion about what it means to act right and tell the truth. Ask: *What does it mean to not hurt a friend and not blame a neighbor? When have you experienced a situation when it was hard to keep your word or to stand up for something that is unpopular with the world?*

Close the Session

❏ Designate a time of silence and ask the group members to find places in the room where they can spend a few minutes in prayer. Encourage them to pray about whatever God may have spoken to them through the Scriptures.

❏ After several minutes of silence, have someone lead in several worship songs. If you don't have someone who can play guitar, play some worship CDs that the students are familiar with.

❏ Close the session with a time of group prayer.

Learning Activity
Worship Through Art

Before the Session

❏ Gather various art supplies for the students to use. These could include: watercolors, colored pencils, crayons, markers, clay, colored chalk, paintbrushes, etc.

❏ Purchase craft paper so that each student can have a large sheet.

❏ Set up tables and chairs for the students to sit around as they arrive for the meeting.

❏ Arrange the art supplies in the middle of the tables.

During the Session

❏ As students arrive, have them find a place at one of the tables where they can work on an art project. Tell the students they will use their creative juices for this meeting. Give students pieces of art paper. Ask them to spend some time creating art pieces that reflect the theme When God sees me, I think He sees . . . (from www.nailscars.com). Allow 15–20 minutes for the students to work. If some students refuse to draw, encourage them to write a creative essay that goes with the theme.

❏ When time is up, ask for volunteers to share what they have created. Don't pressure anyone who doesn't feel comfortable sharing. This will be a very personal project and some students won't feel like showing everyone their art.

❏ Lead in a time of discussion about the obstacles in our lives that can prevent us from experiencing true worship with God. Refer back to the list made during the Bible study option from Psalm 15. Ask students: *What obstacles do teenagers face that would keep them away from God?*

❏ Allow time for discussion. After a few moments, ask the students: *What can a teenager do to remove these obstacles?*

❏ Allow time for responses.

Close the Session

❑ Have students pair off and spend time praying for each other. After five minutes, challenge the students to be accountable to each other during the week.

❑ Encourage each partner to pray for the other during the week. Also ask each student to do something unexpected for his partner during the week. This might be sending him a note, writing a prayer for him and sticking it in his locker at school, spending time together going to a movie or a coffee shop, or giving him a call and checking on him. Explain that sometimes we just need to be held accountable and know someone cares about us and the choices we make each day.

❑ Close the session by praying for each student and the obstacles they face in their daily lives.

Ministry/Witnessing
Leading in Worship

Before the Session

❑ Secure a location where the youth can lead in a worship service. This might be at a retirement home, homeless shelter, children's hospital, etc.

❑ Collect various worship books and resources for the students to use during this activity. These might include worship CDs, hymnals, worship idea books, Bibles, drama books, story books, etc.

❑ Make four signs on poster board that say: *Drama, Art, Dance, Music.* Post the signs on four different walls of the room. If possible, put each group in a separate room to work.

❑ Gather several CD players for students to use during their planning.

During the Session

❑ Tell students they will plan a worship service for the location you have previously determined. Point out the four signs on the walls. Explain that each sign represents a different worship team. Ask students to choose one of the four teams to participate in for this activity.

❑ As students choose their teams, tell them they will plan a part of a worship service they will lead on the day you have arranged. Tell students the worship service theme will be the same as what they have been studying: preparing yourself for worship. Students can plan to do whatever they like within the realm of their particular worship team. Encourage each team to involve every member of their group as they lead in worship. Give teams 30 minutes to plan.

Close the Session

❑ Have each team present their plan for worship. Give guidance to each team as they make their final decisions. Make sure each team plans for 10–15 minutes of worship time.

❑ Have each team make a list of supplies they will need and designate one or two people from the group to be in charge of gathering those supplies.

❑ Set up a time for the groups to meet again to go over the service and then to go and lead in worship.

❑ End the session in prayer for those who will lead in worship and those who will participate in worship.

Cultural Experience
Worship Around the World

Before the Session

❑ During this session, youth will learn how people of other cultures worship God. Invite a retired or visiting missionary to come and share about experiences with worship within a different culture. If there is not a missionary available, invite someone who has been on a missions trip or a college student who has experienced summer missions overseas. If none of these options are available, get an email address of a missionary you could correspond with about experiences with worship.

❑ Purchase an inflatable world globe or a rubber ball that will represent the world.

During the Session

❑ As students enter, have appropriate ethnic music playing to set the mood. After everyone is settled, introduce your speaker for the session. Tell the students they will be hearing from someone who has experienced worship in another culture. Encourage the speaker to not only share a story, but to also lead in an activity or experience where the students will understand firsthand about worship in another culture. If the culture worships through music, play music. If they dance, have the missionary teach a simple dance. If they worship through reading Scriptures, have them read Scriptures in the native language. Ask the speaker to provide as many hands-on activities as possible for the students to experience during the session.

Close the Session

❑ Have everyone sit in a circle. Toss the globe around the circle. As a student catches the globe, have her share a prayer request for the world.

❑ Ask a student to lead in a short prayer for each request given.

❑ After a few moments of passing the globe and praying, ask the missionary to close the session in prayer for the people group she worked with on her missions assignment.

Missionary Ministry
Doug and Darla Millar (Cancun, Mexico)

Before the Session

❑ Plan to hold this session at a Mexican restaurant. If that is not convenient, invite students to a Mexican dinner prepared by volunteers in the church. Serve chips and salsa, tacos, and Mexican wedding dessert (p. 33).

❑ Become familiar with the story of the Millars (p. 34). Be prepared to tell the missionary story in your own words.

❑ Have pen and paper available for three groups to use during the session.

❑ Check the Cancun Fellowship Web site for current prayer requests: www.cancunfellowship.com.

During the Session

❑ After students have enjoyed their dinner, begin the session with the story of the Millars' work in Cancun.

❑ After telling the story of the Millars, divide the students into three teams. Assign each team a people group to consider (p. 33). Ask the students to think about their particular group and come up with a description of that group They will follow the model of "Cancun Carlos." Have them name their character and come up with at least ten descriptive sentences that explain the characteristics of the individuals in their groups.

❑ Give students ten minutes to come up with their descriptions. Have them continue the project by planning an evangelistic event that would attract their group to the church.

❑ Have students share their descriptions and their plans for an evangelistic event. Relate this activity to what the Millars are doing in their ministry in Cancun. Explain that through the description of "Cancun Carlos," the Millars are able to plan their worship services to meet the needs of the people in their area.

Close the Session

❑ Serve Mexican Wedding Dessert.

❑ Close the session with a group prayer that addresses the current prayer requests of the Millars from their Web site: www.cancunfellowship.com.

MEXICAN WEDDING DESSERT

1½ cups flour

1½ sticks butter

4 ounces cream cheese

2 small French vanilla pudding mixes and required milk

1½ cups chopped nuts

1 cup powdered sugar

3 cups whipped topping

First layer: Melt butter in a 9-by-13 pan. Mix in flour and 1 cup nuts. Press the mixture into the bottom of the pan. Bake for 20 minutes at 350°F. Allow the crust to cool for one hour.

Second layer: Mix powdered sugar and cream cheese. Fold in 1½ cups of whipped topping. Spread the mixture over the first layer.

Third layer: Prepare the vanilla pudding according to package directions. Pour over the second layer.

Fourth layer: Top the dessert with remaining whipped topping and sprinkle with nuts.

Group One

People Group:
The senior class at your high school

1. Describe your people group.

2. Following the model of "Cancun Carlos," develop a character to represent your people group.

   a. Name your character.

   b. List at least ten descriptive sentences that explain the characteristics of the individual.

Group Two

People Group:
The athletes at your high school

1. Describe your people group.

2. Following the model of "Cancun Carlos," develop a character to represent your people group.

   a. Name your character.

   b. List at least ten descriptive sentences that explain the characteristics of the individual.

Group Three

People Group:
The artsy kids at your high school

1. Describe your people group.

2. Following the model of "Cancun Carlos," develop a character to represent your people group.

   a. Name your character.

   b. List at least ten descriptive sentences that explain the characteristics of the individual.

Doug and Darla Millar
Cancun, Mexico

Doug and Darla Millar are missionaries to Cancun, Mexico. As church planters, they have a vision to see the people of Mexico come to know the saving power of Jesus.

God gave Doug a vision to start three different kinds of churches: traditional churches, house churches, and larger impact churches. Currently the Millars are working toward growing a church that focuses on reaching the middle and upper classes of Cancun. They have done several different things to attract people to their services. They had Dr. Harold Finch, a scientist from the Apollo Project at NASA, come and speak to reach out to the professional crowd. Then they had the 2001 Super Bowl champion Baltimore Ravens come to work in the area for a week. It was a success and the church is continuing to grow and reach people of the area.

The Cancun Fellowship church is a bilingual church. The church has four weekend services with about 300 people in attendance each week. They hold small group meetings throughout the week to promote fellowship, worship, and discipleship among members. The church meets in a movie theatre. They use upbeat music and have an international praise team. The members of the praise team are from all over the world!

Doug serves as one of the five pastors of Cancun Fellowship. He preaches each Sunday and also leads a small group during the week. Darla serves as a small group leader with women. She also leads the children's ministry.

The people of the Millars' target group are primarily Spanish speaking. This particular area was not heavily populated 30 years ago. It is considered a new land, with new people. Cancun Fellowship was created to reach a particular type of person known as "Cancun Carlos." The information gathered about "Cancun Carlos" helps the church decide what needs to be done to reach that particular part of the population.

"Cancun Carlos"

- I am a newcomer to Cancun
- I work 10 hours/day, 6 days/week
- I do not think I have time for church
- The Bible is true; I know this because my grandmother who cannot read told me so
- I eat at least two meals a day at the hotel where I work
- I often stay on the job longer than they need me (with no pay for the extra time), because the hotel where I work has air-conditioning and they will feed me
- The hotel bus takes me to work each morning at 5:00 A.M.
- I am looking for a better job in the tourism industry
- I am in my twenties
- I am Catholic, but I do not go to church
- I want to learn to speak English better
- I need to find a better house to rent
- If I could only buy land, I would build a house for my family
- I love to play football and basketball on my day off
- We are building the new Mexico
- We are pioneers making a new city
- We love to party and have a good time
- We came here looking to the future (but now some of us just want to survive)
- Connections and friends are the measure of success
- If my friend has it, it is mine
- The boss or company is rich and if I take a little they will not miss it
- All government is corrupt; if they were not, they would give us more

5

Unit 5
Discovering Personal Worship

Introduction
Experiencing True Worship

"When you follow the trail of your time, energy, affection, and money, you will find a throne. And whatever or whoever is on the throne is the object of worship."—Louie Giglio

What is on your throne? Are you so busy with work and family that you have forgotten what true worship is?

I remember the first time I experienced "true worship." I was attending a Passion conference in Fort Worth, Texas. I was surrounded by thousands of college students engrossed in singing and praising God. Hands were raised to the heavens and students were absorbed in worship. The worship leader had introduced a new praise song titled, "Better Is One Day." I'm not sure I can explain it in words, but it felt like the ceiling of the place was going to blow off and we would all be taken home to heaven. It was amazing. I remember thinking, "Where have I been? This is the kind of worship I want to experience all the time!"

Unfortunately, we don't allow ourselves to worship in that manner every time we come before God. We assume someone might think we are strange if we lift our hands. They might ridicule us if we cry because the song was so powerful. They might talk about us at the lunch table if we go to the altar to pray. Our own personal hang-ups keep us from experiencing true worship with our Savior.

This unit will lead students to evaluate their own style of worship. They will learn about corporate worship and the importance of lifting one another up through encouragement. They will explore the meaning of worship and the importance of worshiping in spirit and in truth.

Bible Study
How Do You Worship?

Before the Session

❏ Scatter towels or pieces of construction paper or poster board on the floor throughout your meeting room. Each of these will serve as a marker for where students should sit throughout this activity—one marker per student. Be sure to provide adequate space between the markers so each student has their own space.

❏ Bring a CD player and quiet music to be played during the opening activity.

❏ Make a sign that reads *Enter silently* and tape it to the entrance door of your meeting room. Ask an adult volunteer to stand outside the door to remind students to enter silently.

During the Session

❏ As the students enter the room, have candles lit and soft music playing. Direct the students to find a place to sit on the floor on one of the markers you have placed prior to the activity. Students can sit on any marker and face in any direction.

❏ Welcome the students to this time of worship. Begin the worship time by leading in a prayer, thanking God for the opportunity to worship Him. Ask God's blessing on your worship and for focused minds and the ability to block out distractions throughout the worship experience.

❏ Continue with worship as you lead the students in singing familiar choruses or hymns. If you prefer, prepare several students in advance to each lead one or more choruses. Encourage the group to feel free to close their eyes and focus on God as they sing.

- Ask students to think about someone who is special to them. Encourage the students to think of three reasons they love that person. Give the students time to pray for the special person who is on their mind.

- Ask the students to think about a person sitting near them. Guide the students to see that person as their family or another loved one sees them. Direct the youth to think about the following questions: *What are the best qualities of that person? What strengths do they bring to the group? What concerns do you think this person might be facing?* Give the students an opportunity to pray for the person they have been thinking about.

- Ask the students to stand and form a circle, holding hands. Direct the students to keep their eyes open and have a time of sentence prayers. Guide the students to pray aloud for one another and for the group.

- Have a volunteer read Hebrews 10:24–25 (NIV). Ask students: *What does it mean to spur one another on toward love and good deeds?*

- Allow a few minutes for discussion. Ask: *What types of things can we do to encourage one another in our walks with Christ?*

- Allow time for discussion.

Close the Session

- Ask the students to form one circle. Invite one student to sit in the middle and close his or her eyes. Tell the students you are going to lead them in an encouragement activity. One at a time, each student will take a turn sitting in the middle of the circle. As they sit in the circle, those on the outside of the circle will take turns saying one or two words that describe the person in the middle. Make sure the students understand that this is a time of encouragement. The words they say to describe the person in the middle of the circle should be positive. If your group is large, divide the group and have two encouragement circles.

- After everyone has had a chance to sit in the middle, ask a student to lead the group in a closing prayer.

Learning Activity
Preparing Your Heart for Worship

This activity can be done during a retreat setting or during a normal meeting time. The students will be challenged to explore what the meaning of worship is and how they are called to worship God in spirit and in truth.

Before the Session

- Print the following definition for worship on several note cards: *Worship is our response, both personal and corporate, to God—for who He is and what He has done—expressed in and by the things we say and the way we live* (from www.worship.com). Choose four students to read the definition during the service. Print the definition on a poster board or Power Point slide large enough for the whole group to read.

- Invite someone to come and lead the group in praise and worship. Consider bringing in a college student or young adult to lead during this time. If you don't have someone available in your church to lead this time, consider inviting another youth group to be a part of the retreat and ask if they have someone that can lead in worship. If all else fails, choose some popular worship CDs to use during this time.

- Purchase or borrow the CD *Casting Crowns* (Beach Street Records 2003). Make sure you have access to a CD player.

- Purchase black cotton material. Cut a 1-by-1-foot square for each worship participant. Snip the middle of each square so that it will be easy to tear in half at the appropriate time during the service.

- Select several students to read Scriptures during the service. Choose students to read the Scriptures with feeling and emotion.

- Set up the meeting room with candles that will be burning as the students enter. If available, place a cross at the front of the meeting space. Place two lecterns at the front of the room, one on each side of the meeting area for Scripture readers.

- Provide a nail for each student.

- Pray for God's presence during the service.

During the Session

(Adapted from a worship service at www.nailscars.com/cross_worship.htm)

❏ As students enter, have candles burning, lights dimmed, and soft music playing. After everyone is seated, immediately begin the worship time. Follow the suggested outline for worship or tailor the service to the needs of your students.

Song Set 1

"Come, Now Is the Time to Worship"
"Here I Am to Worship"

Reading 1

Have three preselected students stand from where they are sitting in the audience and read the definition of worship that has been written on an index card. The fourth student will walk to the lectern and ask the group to say the definition together in unison.

Song Set 2

"Open the Eyes of My Heart"
"The Heart of Worship"

❏ Scripture Reading: Isaiah 53:3–6 and Luke 23:45–47

❏ Share a brief explanation about the significance of the ripping of the veil. Then say something like: *Have you ever felt left out? Sometimes we feel separated from God either because we don't feel good enough, smart enough, or pretty enough. But because of the cross we have access to God.*

   Spend a few minutes thinking about what it feels like to be left out in the cold. You may feel like you are separated from God. If that is the case, pray about why you feel that way. Then as you pray, tear your veil in half. Then thank God for opening the way for you to be with Him.

❏ Play the song "Who Am I" by Casting Crowns. If you have someone who signs or dances, ask her to prepare an interpretation of this song to share while it is played. If not, ask students to close their eyes and listen to the words of the song.

❏ Scripture Reading: Ephesians 2:1–9 and Psalm 139

❏ Prayer Needs: Ask students who have a prayer need to stand. As they stand, ask for students who are sitting around them to stand and put their hands on the one who is asking for prayer. Ask them to pray for the person and whatever they are struggling with at that time. Have soft music playing in the background.

❏ Closing Song: "Breathe" (As students sing, invite them to reflect on how God has moved during the service. Invite them to come to the altar or kneel at their seats for prayer. Make sure adult counselors are available for counsel during this time.)

Close the Session

❏ As students leave, give them a nail to remind them of the cross and the gift we have been given through Jesus' death. Have students leave quietly and reverently.

Ministry/Witnessing
Missions: A Response to Worship

Before the Session

❏ Provide poster board and markers for each group to use during the activity.

❏ Gather information from your church, local association, state convention, state WMU office, or missions agency about opportunities for youth to be involved in missions. This information can also be obtained by searching the Internet.

During the Session

❏ Divide the students into four small groups. Do this by writing the names of different people in your church, churches in your association, states, and countries on strips of paper. As students enter, have them draw out a strip of paper from a hat. Have students mingle around and figure out which group they belong to by calling out either a name, association, state, or country. Once they have found their group, they will be given further instructions.

PROJECT IDEAS

Church
- Yard work for elderly church members
- Parents' night out
- Painting the nursery or other Sunday School space
- Car wash for church members
- Adopt a single parent family

Community
- Backyard Bible Club at the city park
- Area-wide yard sale for missions
- Participate in an associational missions trip
- Volunteer at a Christian Women's Job Corps site

State
- Participate in a MissionsFEST celebration
- Plan a missions trip to a resort area in your state
- Visit a children's home and plan activities for the children

International
- Go on a partnership trip with the state convention
- Contact missions agencies and find out areas of the world where youth can volunteer
- Collect and send supplies to a missionary
- Sponsor a child in an underprivileged nation

❏ Tell the groups that they will decide on their missions projects for the coming year. Explain that they will perform four major missions projects during the year: a church project, a community or associational project, a state missions project, and an international project. Each of the four groups will spend 30 minutes brainstorming missions projects that will touch each of the four areas. Each group must not only give ideas, but also include how the group could accomplish the task.

❏ After 30 minutes, have each group take 5 minutes to make presentations. After each presentation, allow 5 minutes for questions from the entire group. Before the presenting group sits down, have the whole group vote on the project they will plan to accomplish for the coming year. See project ideas on page 38.

Close the Session

❏ Divide the group into planning groups for each of the four projects. Have each group brainstorm ideas to plan the missions projects. Instruct each group to select a project planner to act as the organizer for the project. That person will work with the adult leader and her team to put the details together.

❏ End the session with a time of prayer for the projects the students will perform in the coming year.

Cultural Experience
Understanding Other Worship Styles

Before the Session

❏ Call your associational office or another community ministry agency to see if there are churches of a different nationality that worship nearby. Call the pastor of the church and ask if your group can come and worship with them. Set up a time that is convenient for both groups to meet together. Be sure to ask the pastor what to expect regarding appropriate dress and the participation of the youth during the service.

❏ Arrange for transportation to the worship service for your group.

During the Session

❏ During this session, students will have the opportunity to experience worship with another culture. As you plan for the worship experience, prepare your students by teaching them about the culture of the group you will join in worship. Inform students about appropriate dress and behavior during the service.

❏ Before attending the service, ask your students to be prepared to discuss what they experience. Have them think about the following questions:
  • What was different about this worship service and a typical worship service at our church?

- What did you like? What did you not like?
- How was the service similar to our services?
- How was it different?
- How do you think missionaries feel when they go to a foreign land and have to find a place to worship?

Close the Session

❏ Once you arrive back at your meeting place (or on the ride back), lead in a discussion about how the students felt about the experience. Use the questions mentioned above to spark conversation. Brainstorm ways your church could help the other church in their ministry. Have the students commit to do one project that would benefit a ministry of the church they visited.

Missionary Ministry
Jeff Ford (Foley, Alabama)

Before the Session

❏ Plan to hold this session on an indoor volleyball court. Be sure that a volleyball net and ball are available to play the game. If you do not have access to an indoor volleyball court, set up your meeting room to play sock volleyball. String a piece of yarn across the room and secure with strong tape. Bring balloons to serve as the volleyball.

❏ Cut out footprints from construction paper. Write one of the following prayer requests on each footprint:

• Pray for volunteer summer missions teams and summer missionaries.

• Pray for Jeff's wife, Thea, and her work with Gulf Coast High School students.

• Pray for Jeff as he continues his education.

• Pray for summer festivals and the volunteers that will be sharing the gospel with visitors.

❏ Read the story about Jeff Ford (p. 40). Be prepared to tell the story in your own words.

During the Session

❏ Begin the session by playing a game of volleyball. If you do not have access to an indoor volleyball court, play sock volleyball. Divide your group into two teams. Have each team take off their shoes and take their positions at their assigned side of the net. Students will have to sit on the ground and use only their feet to hit the balloon over the "net." Points are scored the same as in a regular volleyball game. Have teams play to 10.

❏ Share the story of Jeff Ford's ministry and the fact that he uses the game of beach volleyball to meet people and share the story of Jesus.

Close the Session

❏ Give each student a footprint with a prayer request from Gulf Coast Resort Ministries. Ask students to get in groups of three to pray over the requests.

Jeff Ford

How beautiful are the feet of those who bring good news. Romans 10:15 is the theme verse for Barefoot Believers, a resort ministry to the Gulf Coast of Alabama. Jeff Ford serves as the director of Gulf Area Resort Ministries. As director of the ministry, his job includes chaplaincy to campgrounds and hotels, leadership in summer and spring break evangelism, campus ministry, and ministry events at area festivals. The purpose of the ministry is to take Christ's message of love to people in leisure settings and vacation spots.

Jeff explains there are many times when a person who wouldn't set foot in a worship service will feel comfortable attending a beach worship service in their shorts and flip flops. The resort setting allows people to hear the gospel message in a casual, nonthreatening setting.

The ministry has a consistent presence each Sunday morning at many area campgrounds. Posters hung up throughout the campgrounds encourage people to come dressed casually for a special time of worship. Those who attend may encounter a youth group sharing in song, drama, puppets, or mime. Other worship services might be held on the beach as the sun is setting. "With an acoustic guitar, leading worship is an awesome blessing," says Jeff.

Jeff depends heavily on the help and support of youth missions teams to volunteer during their spring and summer breaks.

Jeff is quick to mention how youth can get more involved with missions. Resort ministries are all over the US where youth groups can plan a missions trip to go and serve. These include the Smokey Mountains; Big Sky, Montana; Orlando, Florida; Myrtle Beach, South Carolina; Daytona Beach, Florida; Lake Tahoe, California; and Lake Placid, New York. Whether you like the scenic mountains or the sandy beaches, there is a place in resort missions for you to serve!

Unit 6
Discovering Authentic Worship

Introduction
Authentic Worship

Have you ever watched *Antiques Roadshow* on PBS? The popular TV show has avid collectors from around the world bringing in items they hope are valuable for appraisal by antique experts. The best part of the show is when someone brings in a painting or a toy they bought at a yard sale for one dollar only to find out it is valued at thousands of dollars!

The appraisers on the show base an antique's value on its authenticity. Is there some identifiable aspect that proves the item is real?

In this unit, students will discuss what authentic worship means. What makes worship real? Unfortunately, only the individual can identify whether he or she is experiencing authentic worship. There are no worship experts to judge. Many have mastered the ability to fake worship, but God knows our hearts. He knows when we have come with an open and willing spirit to meet with Him.

So many times, we worship out of a sense of obligation. It is part of our normal Sunday routine to get up, put on our Sunday best, drive to church, sit through a service, and then go home feeling as if we have fulfilled our weekly worship duty. God offers so much more to us. He wants to have a real relationship with us. He doesn't just want us to spend time with Him out of obligation or guilt.

These lessons will challenge students to experience real worship. Students will be confronted to evaluate their own worship habits and will be asked to get real with God.

Bible Study
Blind Worship

Before the Session
- ❑ Read through John 4 and become familiar with the story.
- ❑ Invite a woman from your church to prepare a monologue about the woman at the well mentioned in John 4. Have her dress as the woman and tell the story in first person.
- ❑ Gather enough blindfolds for each student to have one to wear.

During the Session
- ❑ As students arrive, have them sit quietly. Dim the room lights and place a spotlight on the front of the room where the monologue will take place. Start the monologue immediately. After the monologue, ask the following questions to start the discussion: *Why do you think Jesus stopped at the well that day? What significance does this story have for us today?*
- ❑ Read John 4:19–26 aloud. Ask: *How does Jesus tell us we should worship?*
- ❑ Make sure students discuss the meaning of "in spirit and in truth." Ask: *Did Jesus say a certain style of worship is best? What does Jesus say about the importance of the way believers worship?*
- ❑ Ask: *How do you feel most comfortable worshiping God? Are there times during worship or in doing other activities that you feel closer to God than others?*
- ❑ Ask for volunteers to share their answers. Ask: *Are you ever afraid to express your worship at church? Why or why not?*
- ❑ Allow time for discussion.

- ❏ Give each student a blindfold. Ask students to spread out in the room so that each will have plenty of space for any movement and then instruct them to put on the blindfolds. Tell students you are going to play several worship songs and you want them to feel free to worship in any way they like. If they want to sing, let them sing. If they want to raise their hands, let them raise their hands, etc. Encourage the students to be free in their worship.

Close the Session

- ❏ After playing a couple of songs, close the time of worship in prayer asking God to allow each person to feel free to worship Him in whatever way they feel most comfortable.

(Idea adapted from "Blind Worship" at www.egadideas.com.)

Learning Activity
Discovering My Worship Style

Before the Session

- ❏ Make five signs on poster board with the following words printed on them: *music, dance/creative movement, drama, art, creative writing*. Tape the signs on the wall in five different areas of the meeting room.
- ❏ At each of the areas, place the following items:
  Music—CD player and a popular contemporary Christian song about worship
  Dance/Creative Movement—CD player and a popular contemporary Christian praise song
  Drama—A paper bag filled with various small items. Include a piece of paper with a theme they must present using the items in the paper bag.
  Art—Paper sack filled with various art supplies, Bible, and Scripture verse about worship.
  Creative Writing—Bible and Scripture verse that focuses on worship (the Psalms are full of verses that pertain to worship), writing paper, and pens.

During the Session

- ❏ Begin the session with a discussion of worship styles. Ask students to identify the worship style of their church. Is it traditional, contemporary, blended, etc? Ask: *If you could plan a Sunday morning worship service, what would you do?*
- ❏ Allow time for discussion.
- ❏ Explain to students that God can be worshiped in many ways. He created each of us as unique individuals with various talents and personalities. Therefore, He also created in us different preferences when it comes to worship.
- ❏ Direct the students' attention to the five signs on the wall. Ask them to consider each worship style and then go sit beneath the sign that reflects their worship preference. Explain that each group will spend a few minutes coming up with an act of worship to share with the rest of the group. At each station there will be a song, Scripture, or idea that will direct them as they work. Give the groups 20 minutes to come up with a way to express their worship style to the larger group.
- ❏ Allow each group to share their presentation with the larger group.

Close the Session

- ❏ Have each of the five groups form a circle. Ask them to share their prayer requests with one another and have one person close in prayer.

Ministry/Witnessing
Plan a Worship Service

Before the Session

- ❏ Invite your music minister to come to your meeting and talk about how to plan a worship service.
- ❏ Contact a retirement center, homeless shelter, campground, hospital chapel, day-care center, or other location to set up a time when your group can lead in a worship service. Plan to go to three different locations, each with a different type of audience.

❏ Gather hymnals, Bibles, CD player and worship CDs, drama books, and other worship aids to be used during the planning.

During the Session

❏ Divide students into three small groups. Assign each of the groups one of the following age divisions: senior adult, middle age, and youth/school-aged children. Instruct each group to plan a worship service that would be appropriate for the particular age grouping. Make sure each group includes music, Scripture, prayer, and a devotional in their service. Other elements may be included, but these four must be a part of the plan. Allow students 30 minutes to plan their worship services.

❏ Have students share their ideas with the larger group. Allow the groups to work together to critique the ideas and create worship services appropriate for each age group. Assign responsibilities to each group member. Practice each service before going to the locations to lead in worship.

❏ Lead the group to pray for the worship services and for those who will take part in them through leadership as well as participation.

Close the Session

❏ After each worship service, conclude with a time of sharing in the group. What did they experience? How did they see God at work? Did the audience respond to the worship style they presented? Why or why not? What would they do differently next time?

Cultural Experience
Leading Others in Worship

Before the Session

❏ During this session, students will plan a worship service designed to lead their congregation in experiencing different worship styles.

❏ Plan a time with your pastor when the youth can lead the congregation in worship.

❏ Gather poster board and markers for students to use for planning.

During the Session

❏ Have a poster board mounted on the wall at the front of the meeting room. Ask students to tell you what part of the study of worship they have enjoyed the most. Write their responses on the poster board.

❏ Tell students they will be reflecting on the sessions of the past three months and what they have learned about worship. Explain in this session, that the group will plan a worship service designed to lead their church congregation to a greater understanding of worship and worship in other cultures.

❏ Take 10 minutes to brainstorm elements of worship the students would like to include in their service. Remind them that the service should reflect a combination of traditional, contemporary, and cultural elements of worship. After the brainstorming session is complete, have the students divide into several groups. The groups should focus on music, prayer, Scripture, or devotion. Tell each group to plan their assigned section around the theme of worship. Encourage the groups to be creative as they plan.

❏ After 20 minutes, bring the groups back together to create one worship service that will last about one hour. Have each group present their ideas and then have the group as a whole work together on how the service will flow and the timing of each element. After the worship elements have been put in order, assign tasks to each student and set a time when the group can come back together to practice the service.

Close the Session

❏ Lead the group in a time of prayer, remembering the worship service they will lead for the congregation.

Missionary Ministry
Connie Pearson (Ecuador)

Before the Session

❏ Plan to hold this session in a kitchen.

❏ Gather the needed supplies to make Ecuadorian Potato and Cheese Patties (Llapingachos) with Peanut Sauce (p. 45). (From www.prochef.com)

❏ Read through the story of Connie Pearson. Be prepared to tell her story in your own words.

During the Session

❏ As students arrive direct them to the kitchen. Explain that today's missionary is Connie Pearson. She serves with her husband in Ecuador. Although Connie serves in many different ways, her most prominent job is to serve others through hospitality and teaching.

❏ Explain that during today's session, the group will be making Ecuadorian Potato and Cheese Patties (Llapingachos) with Peanut Sauce. After the treat is finished, they will invite other church members to share their appetizer.

❏ Begin by having students peel potatoes and cook them. During the cooking process, tell the story of Connie Pearson (p. 46).

❏ After you have shared the story, continue to make the Llapingachos and Peanut Sauce.

Close the Session

❏ Have students invite church members to come and share the Llapingachos and peanut sauce. Have students share with their guests about the Pearsons and the work they are doing in Ecuador.

❏ Close the session in prayer for the Pearsons. Have someone lead the prayer, but ask everyone else to pray at the same time in a lower voice. Remind students that this is a practice of the Quichua people in their worship.

Ecuadorian Potato and Cheese Patties with Peanut Sauce

LLAPINGACHOS

[yah-peen-GAH-chos]

(Potato and Cheese Patties)

4 medium russet potatoes, peeled and
   quartered

2 quarts water

1 tablespoon coarse salt

6 Scallions, finely minced

4 ounces Monterey Jack Cheese, grated

½ teaspoon black pepper

¼ teaspoon salt to taste

½ cup corn oil

peanut sauce

Place the potatoes in a medium pot with the water and 1 tablespoon salt. Bring to a boil on high heat. Simmer until soft, about 30 minutes. Drain and mash, leave the mixture slightly chunky.

When the potatoes cool a bit, add the scallions, cheese, and black pepper. Mix well. Divide the potatoes into 24 balls—about one heaping tablespoon of potatoes for each ball. Flatten the balls to form patties. Make the patties about 1½ inches thick. Let them cool for at least 20 minutes before cooking; otherwise they will stick to the pan and fall apart.

Heat a 10-inch skillet. Add the corn oil. Allow the oil to heat through. Place the patties in the pan and cook for 3 minutes on low heat to form a crust. Flip the patties over and brown on the other side.

Serve hot with a dollop of peanut sauce.

PEANUT SAUCE

3 ounces roasted unsalted peanuts

½ cup whole milk

3 tablespoons corn oil

1 medium white onion, finely chopped

4 garlic cloves, finely chopped

½ teaspoon cumin

½ teaspoon pepper

1 teaspoon salt

¾ cup water

½ teaspoon lime juice

¼ cup chopped cilantro

Place the peanuts and milk in a blender or food processor; process into a smooth puree. Set aside. Heat the oil over medium heat in a small skillet or saucepan. Add the onion and sauté until light golden. Add the garlic, and sauté until light golden. Add cumin, pepper, and salt and continue to sauté until aromatic.

Add the peanut puree and stir. Cook, stirring until thick and creamy. Add lime juice and dilute with water until it has a sauce consistency. Top with cilantro.

Connie and Steve Pearson
Missionaries to Ecuador

Connie and Steve Pearson are missionaries to Ecuador. Steve is a veterinarian who helps educate the local people about their livestock and other animals. Connie teaches English and music. Both of them have been called to share the gospel through worship, prayer, and teaching.

The Pearsons work with the Quichua people group who live in the Andes Mountains of Ecuador. The Quichua people have been oppressed for many years. Many were even considered to be slaves and of the lowest class for over 600 years. It is only recently that they have achieved some political rights in the country.

The Pearsons feel strongly about the power of prayer and worship. During a recent prayerwalking experience, they got to see the power of on-site praying! God is at work in Ecuador.

The worship experience in Ecuador is different than what we experience in the US. In Quichua churches, one person may be leading in prayer, but everyone is praying their own prayers aloud at the same time. The Quichua people have a strong desire to see God at work during their worship services. They use their prayertime to implore God to be present. A typical time of praise and worship will last anywhere from 30 minutes to an hour before the preacher begins. It is common for the offering basket to be passed multiple times, depending on the needs of those in the congregation.

Guitars and drums are used in the praise music. Quichua music might sound strange to your ears at first. It is based on a five-tone minor scale and is usually sung in high-pitched voices. The music is upbeat and rhythmic!

The Pearsons live in an apartment in Cuenca, which is the third largest city in Ecuador. Connie has the opportunity to serve others through the ministry of hospitality. She has invited numerous people to come to their home for dinner. She uses the opportunity to get to know people better and establishes relationships with them in hopes that she will have the opportunity to share Christ with them in the future. Cuenca has some modern conveniences, but Connie cannot get many things on a regular basis, such as frozen foods, canned goods, and convenience foods.

The Quichua people have adopted many traditions from the Incas and Roman Catholics. One of the unusual things they eat is *cuy* (pronounced KWEE), or guinea pigs. The animals are served in stews, roasted, or fried. This treat is saved for special guests on special occasions. The Pearsons have learned to eat it all three ways!

Please pray for the Pearsons as they continue to learn the Spanish language and the culture of the Quichua people. Pray for their adult children who live in the US. Pray for continual opportunities to teach and witness through worship and prayer.

Unit 7
The Bible: How Is It Relevant to My Life?

7

Introduction
Striving for Perfection

Christ follower. The words conjure up the image of someone who has it all together. A Christ follower gets up in the morning and reads her Bible. She memorizes Scripture while waiting in traffic. She prays daily for not only her family, but also for the missionaries, the president, her neighbor, and her pastor. A Christ follower is patient and loving at all times. She basically exudes Christ in every situation.

Right! Don't you wish that description were true of each of us who are believers? I wonder what kind of world this would be if Christians actually lived as Christ did? Our churches would be overflowing. People would be serving one another at every opportunity. And yet, that is what we are called to do as Christ followers. We are to strive to be like Christ.

The idea of being like Christ is overwhelming at times. Jesus was so perfect and we are so human. We yell at people in traffic. We get upset when the cable goes out. We let opportunities to tell others about Christ slip by without a second thought. Nevertheless, God forgives us and gives us another chance to get it right.

This unit will lead students to understand the importance of spiritual discipline through Bible study, meditation, and Scripture memorization. Students will be challenged to be in a right and growing relationship with God. They will realize that even though they are not perfect, they are to strive for perfection in their daily walk with Christ.

Bible Study
Using the Bible to Grow as a Christ Follower

Before the Session

❏ Borrow or purchase a large supply of Lego building blocks, enough for at least four small groups—depending on the size of your group—to have enough to create a specific shape. Create a sample shape for each group, and be sure to have diagrams available for how to create each shape. You may want to choose four different shapes, some that are much more difficult than others.

❏ Using a marker, write out the following Scripture references on a piece of poster board that you will cut up and make into a puzzle: Deuteronomy 6:2–3; Joshua 1:8; 2 Timothy 3:16; and 2 Timothy 2:15. Create puzzles for at least 4 groups. If you will have more than four groups, be sure to have more than four Scripture reference puzzles. Keep each of your puzzles separate by placing them in individual plastic baggies. Be sure to write all four Scripture references on the poster board for each puzzle.

❏ Gather 4 pieces of poster board and several markers for each group.

❏ Read through the Scripture references that are mentioned throughout the lesson. Be ready to share your personal thoughts about the importance of studying the Bible.

During the Session

❏ As students arrive, direct them to one of four tables that have been set up for the activity. Tell students they are going to use their collection of Lego building blocks to create the sample you have placed on each table. Do not provide the diagrams to any of the groups for this first attempt to copy the creation. Tell the groups you will give a prize to the groups who complete their structure first. Have bite-sized candy for the students in the group that finishes first.

❏ If you have selected several different structures for the groups, some will likely finish much more quickly than others. Ask: *What did it feel like to try and create this structure without having a diagram to follow? How did it feel to be racing against the other groups when some of the groups had easier structures to build than others? What was challenging about this activity?*

❏ Do the activity again, but provide each group with a diagram showing how to put the structure together. Give a prize to the group who completes their structure first—and eventually you can give a prize to all the groups for attempting a difficult task. Ask: *How much easier was this activity when you had the instructions for how to create the structure? How can these two activities be compared to trying to follow God without studying the Bible?*

❏ Ask the students: *Why is the Bible important? We will look at some specific Scriptures related to studying the Bible. Hopefully, we will all leave today knowing the importance of the Bible to our daily lives.*

❏ Divide the large group into four smaller groups and give each group a baggie with puzzle pieces. Ask the groups to put their puzzles together and then look up the Scripture verses that are listed and read them.

❏ When the groups have completed this assignment, have them come back together. Ask: *How did it feel to put your puzzle together without knowing what it was going to be when you completed it? How can we relate this to our daily lives when we don't study God's Word? After reading these verses, what have you learned about the benefits of studying the Bible?*

❏ Allow each group to share their verses and what they discussed together. Ask leading questions to prompt further discussion as needed.

❏ Direct the students to return to their small groups. Provide each group with a piece of poster board and several markers. Assign each group one of the following passages: Psalm 19; 2 Timothy 3:14–25; James 1:17–27. Ask the groups to read their assigned passage and create billboards that would take what they have learned and encourage others to get into God's Word. Give students a few minutes to work on their billboards and then share them with the large group.

Close the Session

❏ Ask: *Of all the things we have learned today about studying God's Word, what motivates you the most to read the Bible?*

❏ Allow students to respond, and then close the session in prayer. Ask God to give each person there a hunger for studying the Bible.

Learning Activity
Growing with God

Before the Session

(Activity from "Shoes of Faith," www.egadideas.com.)

❏ Gather the following shoes to use during the session: old house shoes, dress shoes, worn-out shoes, sandals, running shoes, work boots, and animal house shoes.

❏ Write the following Scripture references on index cards: Micah 6:8, Ephesians 6:14–15, 1 John 1:5–7, John 8:12, Psalm 89:15, Isaiah 40:29–31, and 2 John 4–6.

❏ Purchase a pair of shoelaces for each student who will participate in the session.

During the Session

❏ Give the Scripture reference cards to seven students. Ask them to read the Scripture aloud. Ask the group to listen closely to figure out how the Scripture verses are related to one another.

❏ After all the verses have been read, allow a few moments for a response and then say: *Many Scriptures refer to walking. God loves to use mental images in the Bible. I think He does this in order to help us understand that our relation-*

ship with God is like taking a walk. Sometimes the road is easy and then sometimes it seems like we just can't take another step. Today we are going to focus on our own walk with God.

❏ Divide the group into seven smaller groups. Give each group a pair of shoes. Ask each group to come up with an analogy, using the pair of shoes that they have been given, to describe someone's walk with God. For example, the running shoes might represent the times when things get tough really quick, but with God's guidance, we can persevere and finish the race.

❏ Allow the groups to work for five minutes and then ask for each group to share their thoughts. Ask: *Which of these shoes best represents your walk with Christ? As Christ followers, we know that we never walk alone. God walks beside us and even carries us whenever it is necessary. He walks with us and makes sure that we don't stumble and fall, but encourages us to carry on.*

Close the Session

❏ Give each student a shoelace with the reference *1 John 1:7* written on it.

❏ Have students use the shoelaces in their shoes to remind them to strive to be Christ followers in every step that they take.

Ministry/Witnessing
Parents' Night Out

Before the Session

❏ Arrange for the youth to go to a community center, day care, or other agency that serves underprivileged children to host a "Parents' Night Out."

❏ Gather children's ministry reference books (Bible stories, crafts, games, etc.).

❏ Set up a flip chart and markers at the front of the meeting area.

❏ Label four large sheets of flip-chart paper with the following headings: *Music, Bible Story/Prayer, Games,* and *Crafts/Snacks.* Place the sheets in different areas of the room with markers for writing.

❏ Place a CD player and children's worship CDs near the music group.

During the Session

❏ Have students gather in a large group at the front of the meeting room. Explain to them that they will be planning and sponsoring a "Parents' Night Out" event. Leading the group in deciding on a theme for the event. After the students decide on a theme, divide the group into four smaller groups. Have each group go to a designated area. Ask each group to decide on activities that will support the theme.

❏ As students work, visit each group and offer guidance. Be sure to let students know about the resources that are available to them as they plan. Allow the groups to work for 25 minutes.

❏ Have each group present their ideas to the large group. Assign each student a particular task to be responsible for during the actual event. Have each group make a list of items that they will need to complete their particular activity.

After the Session

❏ Purchase the needed supplies for the event.

❏ Publicize the event around the neighborhood where it will take place.

❏ Arrange transportation for youth to and from the event.

❏ Put together a step-by-step outline of what is going to happen and who is in charge of each activity. Give each student a copy of the schedule and post one at the front of the meeting room for easy reference.

❏ Ask for adult volunteers to help with the activities. Plan to have one adult for every five students.

❏ Lead the students in a time of prayer before the event.

Cultural Experience
Using Media to Spread the Gospel

Before the Session

(Activity from "Search for God," www.egadideas.com.)

❑ Gather the following items to be used during this session: Bible written in a different language, newspaper, magazine, evangelistic tract, small radio, picture of a TV, and a copy of an Internet page.

❑ Collect enough blindfolds for each student to have one to wear.

❑ Invite a speaker to share with your group about how they use different types of media to reach people for Christ. If you have a Christian radio station in your area, invite a DJ to come and share with the group. If you don't know anyone who could speak on this topic, email a missionary who works with translating the Bible and share the email with your students. Contact a missionary sending organization for a list of missionaries who might be available to speak to this topic.

❑ Purchase a blank CD for each student.

❑ Purchase colored, permanent markers for students to use to decorate their CDs.

During the Session

❑ Begin by playing a game called, "Search for God." Give each student a blindfold to put on. Select one youth to represent God. Be sure that no one knows who has been selected to be "God." Have everyone except "God" leave the room. Bring each person in one at a time. Explain to students that as they enter, they will remain silent and begin to walk around slowly. (You may want to instruct students to cross their arms in front of them to insure that no one gets hurt during this activity.) When a student bumps into another person, each will ask, "Are you 'God'?" If the person is not "God," the response is no, and both will continue to look for "God." If the person is "God," "God" will respond very quietly with a yes. "God" and the seeker will then link arms and become one. As youth find "God," they can remove their blindfolds. The "God" blob will continue to get larger as students find it. Continue the game until everyone has found "God."

❑ When the game is over, ask: *What was it like trying to find God in the dark? Did it seem like it took a long time to find God? How did it feel once you found God?*

❑ Allow time for discussion.

❑ Say: *Each of us went through a time in our lives when we didn't know God. We were essentially bumping into things in the dark and trying to find our way. That is how it is without God to guide us each day. Many people around the world are walking in the dark. That is why it is so important for us to share Christ with our friends, neighbors, family, and the world!*

❑ *Today we are going to explore some ways that we can share Jesus in our own culture.*

❑ Divide the students into seven groups. Give each one of the groups a media object, a piece of flip-chart paper, and a marker. Ask the groups to spend a few minutes brainstorming as many ways as possible that someone could use the item to share Christ with others. Encourage students to include ways that they have seen the media use the particular item they were assigned. Allow each of the groups to share their lists.

❑ Allow time for your guest to share her use of media in sharing the gospel. Invite students to ask questions at the end of the session.

Close the Session

❑ Give each student a blank CD. Have students decorate the CD using permanent colored markers. Have them decorate the CD in a way that will remind them to pray for those who share the love of God through different types of media.

❑ Encourage the students to display the CD in a place where they can see it each day.

Missionary Ministry
Stan and Pam Wafler (The Sudan, Africa)

Before the Session

❏ Provide the following translations of the Bible to be used in the session: New International Version, King James Version, *The Message*, and The New Living translation.

❏ Read through the story of Stan and Pam Wafler (p. 52). Become familiar with their story so that you can tell it in your own words.

During the Session

❏ Begin the session by telling the story of Stan and Pam Wafler.

❏ Lead the group in a time of discussion. Ask the following questions:
  • *Why is Bible translation important?*
  • *Why can't the Waflers just use Bible story-telling and not worry about translating the Bible into the Keliko language?*

❏ Give several students a different translation of the Bible. Have them read John 3:16 from each of the different translations. Have them identify the differences of each translation. Ask: *Which one is the easiest to understand? Did the meaning change in any of the translations?*

❏ Divide the group into groups of three or four. Ask each group to take the verse, John 3:16, and translate it so that their assigned people group will understand its meaning. Assign each group one of the following people groups: preschoolers, 10-year-olds, high school students, college students, and single parents.

❏ Have groups share their translations. Ask: *Was your assignment harder than you thought it would be? What did you have to take into account when translating? Was it easy to maintain the same meaning of the verse in your translation?*

Close the Session

❏ Lead the group in a time of prayer for the Waflers and the work they are doing through Bible translation and storytelling.

Stan and Pam Wafler
Sudan, Africa

Stan and Pam Wafler are missionaries to Sudan, Africa. The Waflers are assigned to work as Bible translators and to share the gospel through chronological storytelling methods. Stan is currently assigned to work with the Keliko translation team. His job is to translate books of the Bible into the Keliko language. Once a book has been translated, the team labors over the translation to make the meaning clear so that people understand.

Sometimes translating the Bible into Keliko presents a problem, such as in Acts 4:11 where Jesus is described as the capstone or cornerstone. In Southern Sudan, houses are not built with stone. Houses are built with wooden poles and mud. A literal translation of this verse would have no meaning to the people. So, the translation team must come up with a way to give the same meaning of the verse, but in terms that the people will understand. In Southern Sudan, people sometimes use a center pole, which will hold the roof and house together. Therefore, in Acts 4:11 of the Keliko Bible, the verse will read, "Jesus is the important pole that the builders rejected and has become the most important center pole that holds the whole house together." Once the team comes up with a good translation, they will go into the villages and read the translation to the people. They will then ask questions to check for the people's understanding. If the people don't understand the meaning, the translators adjust the translation so the people get the right meaning.

In other instances the lifestyle of the Sudanese people is very similar to the Bible. For example, when the team was working on Exodus, they used a verse that refers to unleavened bread used in the Passover. The Keliko culture doesn't use bread, they do not have wheat to make bread, or yeast to allow it to rise. However, they do have a substance that is similar to bread that comes from cornmeal. This substance has no yeast and is referred to as *panga*. *Panga* is a quick snack or travel bread. The team used the word *panga* in the translation because it is exactly the idea of the bread that is used in Exodus. The Bible tells of how the Israelites left Egypt quickly and did not have time to let their bread rise. By using the word *panga* in the translation, the people will immediately understand that the word means quick travel bread.

Another part of the Waflers' assignment is to share the Bible message through oral communication methods such as stories, dramas, and songs. The Keliko alphabet was created in 1998, therefore the people have used oral communication throughout history to pass down their stories. Stan says, "If we wait until everyone can read the translation, most of the Keliko will never understand the gospel. This is true of most of the people in Sudan. Because of the war, the education system has been available on and off for only a few select people for more than 20 years. Using chronological Bible storying is a way to help oral communicators get the message without having to wait for literacy to reach them."

Unit 8
Is the Bible Relevant for Today?

8

Introduction
The Bible: Our Leash on Life

I have a new Chihuahua/Dachshund mix puppy who is named Peanut. She is the cutest little dog. She wags her tail and runs to meet me when I get home. She loves to jump and play with her toys. She is a very happy little dog—that is, until the leash comes out! The minute I get the leash, she goes crazy. She immediately hides behind the couch or under the bed. She hates the leash.

I'm not sure why she hates it. It's a perfectly good leash. It allows her the freedom to walk close or far away. It is an attractive purple color, and she looks so cute with it on as she prances down the road.

I guess the problem starts when she decides she wants to go a different direction than I do. She can only go so far on the leash. It keeps her in line and away from danger. When a car is coming, I press a button on the leash and it stops Peanut in her tracks—I don't think she likes that. She would much rather roam free with no one to stop her or hurry her along. She wants to be in charge of which way she goes.

We tend to be like Peanut when it comes to leashes. We don't like anyone telling us what to do or where to go. We like our freedom. But, as Christ followers, we have a leash that gives us direction. It is the Bible. God chose to give us a book full of information that will help us stay on the right path. If we follow what it says, it will keep us safe and away from danger.

In this unit, students will focus on the relevance the Bible has to their lives. They will learn the benefits of studying the Bible as they seek God's direction. Just as Peanut has learned the importance of walking on a leash, students will learn the importance of reading and memorizing Scripture.

Bible Study
Show Me the Way

Before the Session

❏ Draw a simple picture of a flower and a house on two separate index cards. Make enough cards for every two students to have one of each picture.

❏ Have copy paper and pens available for the beginning activity.

❏ Read the focal Scripture (Psalm 1:2; 119:105) and be ready to lead in a discussion about how God's Word gives us the guidance we need for our daily lives.

❏ Invite a youth worker to share a testimony about how reading God's Word has helped in her daily walk with God.

❏ Purchase a light bulb for each student.

❏ Gather permanent colored markers to be used for the craft activity.

❏ Obtain a large map of the United States and tape it to one wall of your meeting room.

❏ Have a blindfold ready for the map activity.

During the Session

❏ Have students find a partner and sit back to back on the floor. Assign one partner to be the person who will describe and the other to be the one who will draw whatever is described to him or her. Give the describers a picture and tell them that they are to describe the picture to their partners. The persons who are drawing, must draw exactly what the describer tells them to draw. The describer may not tell the person who is drawing what the picture is. For example, the describer cannot say: *Draw a flower.*

- Let students draw for one minute and then have each person show her drawing to the large group. Have students switch roles and draw another picture.
- Ask: *How did you feel when you were the person who was trying to describe the picture? What about when you were the one trying to understand the description? Was it easy to understand what to do? How is this activity like listening to God?*
- Say: *Sometimes listening to God and understanding what He is saying can be very confusing. It would be so much easier if God told us directly what we should do, but many times, He wants us to listen and take small steps toward His plan for our lives. Just like in this activity, it would have been much easier to draw the object if the describer said, "Draw a flower with four round petals, a stem, and one leaf." Instead, I asked you to give directions step by step to draw the flower.*
- Ask a volunteer to read Psalm 119:105 and Psalm 1:2. Ask someone to explain what the verses mean. Share your thoughts about the verses. Focus on the benefits of Bible study and the direction it can give each of us in our daily lives.
- If available, invite the guest speaker to share a testimony about how God has used Scripture to give her direction for life.
- Place a large map of the United States on the wall. One at a time, ask the students the name of the state they would most like to visit. Once each student has responded, place a blindfold on him or her and spin the student around three times. Guide the student to the wall where the map is located and ask the student to place her finger on the state she said she would most like to visit. When the student has pointed to the map, remove the blindfold and let her see where her finger landed. Allow every student to have a turn, time permitting.
- Say: *When we don't allow God to guide us, we usually end up going in the wrong direction. Many people who claim to be Christians don't allow God to lead their lives, not to mention those who have never made a decision to follow Christ. Life is always more full and hopeful when we allow God to lead us. When we find ourselves lost in life, the place to turn for direction and purpose in our lives is God.*

When we follow God's plan for our lives we will find that direction we all desire. Knowing God's plan for us comes from knowing God. We can develop our relationship with God through prayer, Bible study, fellowship with other Christians, and worship, just to name a few. God is always there for us, we just have to call on Him and He will be there.

Close the Session

- Give each student a light bulb and several permanent markers. Ask students to write the reference *Psalm 119:105* on the light bulb. Let the students decorate their light bulbs.
- Tell students to take their light bulbs home and put them in a place where they will see it during the week. Make it clear to students that they cannot use the light bulb.
- Challenge students to memorize the verse for your next meeting time.
- Close the meeting with prayer, thanking God for His guidance in each student's life.

Learning Activity
Road Rules: Mission Style

Before the Session

- Enlist adult drivers for each Road Rules team. Ask for other adult volunteers to help with some of the details of the weekend.
- Make reservations at a place where the whole group can gather for a retreat.
- Make arrangements with area ministries for students to perform a missions project. Plan a different ministry project for each Road Rules group.
- Make a map for each group that gives directions to each destination. Include the appropriate information listed in During the Session.
- Choose five Bible verses that refer to being a servant. Write each word of the verses on a separate index card. Place the index cards for each verse in a separate envelope or plastic baggie. Hide the envelopes in the meeting area that has been designated as stop three.
- Enlist volunteers to lead in worship during the last session.

During the Session

❏ Plan a spring retreat after the popular MTV series *Road Rules.* Do not disclose the location of the retreat to the students. Divide into groups of four or five students.

❏ Give each group their first clue that will lead them to their first destination. Each group will open the clue, drive to the destination, and perform the given task.

❏ Enlist adult volunteers to deliver clues at each stop.

❏ Plan the following stops along the way for students to experience an emphasis on Scripture reading and meditation.

Stop One: Give the group a partial map with directions to their first stop. On the map, write the Scripture reference *John 10:43–45,* and the name of the contact person they are to find. Have the map lead the group to a location where they can do some type of ministry project. Some examples would be to serve breakfast at a homeless shelter, yard work or home repair at an elderly person's home, cleanup and sanitation at a day-care center, etc. Plan each project to last for several hours.

Stop Two: The clue will be delivered by an adult volunteer. It will include another piece of the map that will lead the group to their lunch destination. This could be a restaurant or someone's home. Before students are allowed to eat, they must work as a team to memorize a chapter in the Bible. They may choose to do it in any manner they wish, but they must recite a chapter of the Bible.

Stop Three: After lunch, another clue will be delivered to the team by an adult volunteer. The clue will lead the group to a gym or open field where they can play games. The first task will be for students to find the five prepared hidden envelopes with the scrambled Bible verses. Give the students clues on where to find the envelopes. When they find an envelope, they must unscramble the verse. Plan other games to play during the recreation time.

Stop Four: After an hour, deliver another clue that will lead the groups to their final destination. Before they are allowed to enter the retreat

grounds, have an adult stop the vehicle and make all the students get out. The group will be asked to recite a designated number of Bible verses. Once the students recite the verses, they will be admitted to the retreat center.

Close the Session

❏ Once students are at the retreat site, have a time of debriefing for each activity. Allow each group to share about their ministry experience. Ask students to share their reaction to memorizing a chapter in the Bible and about sharing memory verses before they were allowed to enter the retreat area.

❏ Ask volunteers to share what they learned from the experience.

❏ Plan a time of worship that includes singing, Scripture reading, prayer, and a devotion. Ask a student to share a testimony about how God spoke to him or her through the sessions on Scripture reading and memorization.

Ministry/Witnessing
Literacy Missions

Before the Session

❏ During this session, the Youth on Mission group will be asked to lead the church in a literacy missions project. Do research about the literacy programs already in place in your community. If possible, plan a project that will enhance one of those programs. If there is not any literacy missions work in your community, plan a project that will benefit the local school system, or a day-care center, children's hospital, or children's home.

❏ Gather the following supplies: poster board, markers, masking tape, cardboard boxes, scissors, and wrapping paper.

During the Session

❏ At the beginning of the session, explain to the youth that they will be leading the church in a book drive to support literacy missions in their area. Direct the students' attention to the art supplies that have been gathered. Ask the students to make posters that will be hung around the church to encourage church members to purchase books for children and youth to be donated to the book drive. Make sure students include who will receive the books and when the collection time will be over on each poster.

❏ If you have a computer that is accessible during this time, have a couple of students design a flyer to be included in the bulletin each Sunday for the next couple of weeks.

❏ Have students decorate several boxes with wrapping paper to be placed at various locations in the church for book donations.

❏ Once the books have been collected, plan for a time to deliver the books to the ministry you previously selected. If possible, set up a time when students can go and spend time reading to people. If the books are being donated to a school, students might be able to go to an after school program and spend time reading with the children. If the books are going to a library, set up a story time activity with the librarian that the youth can lead.

❏ Be creative with how the students minister through this project.

Close the Session

❏ Encourage the youth to commit to a literacy missions project for the next three months. Brainstorm ideas that the students can do to promote reading with children, teens, and adults in their community.

Cultural Experience
What Kind of Leader Was Jesus?

Before the Session

❏ Purchase enough modeling clay or play dough for each student to have plenty to create a small sculpture.

❏ Read through the Scriptures that will be used during the lesson.

❏ Gather needed supplies: flip-chart paper and markers

❏ Photocopy "Real Life Scenarios" and cut them apart (p. 59).

During the Session

❏ Give each student a lump of modeling clay or play dough. Ask students to make a sculpture with their clay that will communicate who Jesus was as a leader. Give students five minutes to come up with a sculpture. Allow each student to share her creation with the large group. Ask each student to share the reasoning behind the sculpture.

❏ Divide the students into two groups. Have groups read Mark 10:35–45. Ask each group to be prepared to answer the following questions about the Scripture verses:
   • *Why did James and John ask what they did?*
   • *Why did the other disciples become angry?*
   • *According to these verses, what does Jesus say makes a good leader?*
   • *How do you think Jesus would lead our country today?*
   • *Where would He turn for guidance?*

❏ Give each group a piece of flip-chart paper and a marker. Have one group label their paper with *authoritative leader*. The other group will label their paper with *servant leader*. Ask each group to write down different characteristics of these types of leaders.

❏ After a few minutes, have them post their papers and share with the large group their findings. Ask: *Which one of these leadership styles do you tend to have when you are placed in a leadership position? Is it easier to be an authoritarian leader or a servant leader?*

❏ Give each group a scenario of a real-life situation for them to read and determine how a Christ follower would react in this particular situation.

❏ Ask each group to share their thoughts about how the person in each scenario could change their actions and become a servant leader.

Close the Session

❏ Have the large group make a list of leaders in their lives. The list could include the president, governor, teachers, parents, pastor, youth leader, etc.

❏ Have each student find a partner and spend time praying for each of these leaders, that they might have the courage to lead like Jesus.

Missionary Ministry
Jon Jamison

Before the Session

❏ Pack a travel bag with personal hygiene items that you would use in the morning to get ready for work. Include soap, shampoo, toothbrush, toothpaste, lotion, etc.

❏ Bring a US map and mark Des Moines, Iowa, with a sticker.

❏ Collect several large boxes. Provide wrapping paper, tape, markers, and construction paper for students to use to decorate the boxes.

❏ Read through the story of Jon Jamison and be prepared to tell it in your own words (p. 58).

During the Session

❏ Begin the lesson by pulling out the travel bag. Ask students to list some of the products they use in the morning to get ready for school. Have them explain why they use a particular product. After a few moments, pull out the items that you have packed in the bag. Explain the importance of each item: *I use this brand of shampoo because it helps me keep my frizzy hair under control.*

❏ Explain that many people struggle with providing these everyday items for their families. Many people can't afford a special kind of shampoo or nice perfume. They struggle with paying the electric bill and putting food on the table each night. That is why places such as the Friendship Center in Des Moines, Iowa, were established to help those who need a helping hand.

❏ Tell the story of Jon Jamison.

❏ Say: *The Jamisons are always eager to see youth get involved with missions. How can you help? Volunteer to serve during the summer at a community center like the Friendship Baptist Center. Volunteers are always needed to lead in Backyard Bible Clubs or in day camps.*

If you can't volunteer your time, many ministries always need personal hygiene items. Start a collection of soap, shampoo, tooth-paste, and toothbrushes for a center. Your help may give the center an open door to share the love of Christ with someone in need.

Close the Session

❏ Have students decorate several large boxes to lead the church in a collection of personal hygiene items. Inform the congregation what you are collecting, where the items are going, and how long items will be collected.

❏ Send the items to a community center in your area that ministers to the needs of low-income families.

❏ Close the session in prayer for Jon and Mindy Jamison and the work they do at the Friendship Baptist Center.

Jon and Mindy Jamison
Missionaries in Des Moines, Iowa

Jon and Mindy Jamison are missionaries who serve in Des Moines, Iowa, at the Friendship Baptist Center. The center is an inner-city ministry that focuses on the needs of low-income families. The community where they serve is made up of African American, Hispanic, Bosnian, Sudanese, Vietnamese, and Caucasian people. The ministries that the center provides are intended to meet the physical as well as spiritual needs of those in the community.

Jon and Mindy felt called to inner-city ministry after they both served as social work interns at New Orleans Baptist Theological Seminary. They also both felt a special calling to work as a team in ministry. They didn't know where God would lead them, but they knew He would lead them to a place where they could serve together. God was faithful to His calling and lead the Jamisons to the Friendship Center in Des Moines, Iowa.

Morning ministries at the center include monthly grocery distribution, community clothes closet, conversational English classes, and community worship services. The afternoons are dedicated to serving children and youth through an after-school program. The program is called "Kids Club" and serves children from 4–18 years old. The children play games, have Bible study, and are tutored in their schoolwork.

Another ministry of the center is literacy and English as a second language classes for those who struggle with the English language. Beginner and intermediate classes are available. Volunteers meet one on one with the students who need assistance with literacy and preparation to take the GED. Children are also tutored in reading and language skills.

Through meeting the physical needs of the people in the community, the Jamisons are also given many opportunities to share the gospel message with those they serve. This is evident as you hear the stories of those who have come to know Christ through the ministries of the center. One person who became a Christian as a result of Kids Club is Brandon. Jon describes Brandon as "one who stood out from the very beginning. He was extremely bright, a great athlete, and had a great sense of humor." Brandon didn't go to church and he knew very little about God. Through the children's ministries of the center, Brandon quickly learned about Jesus and that He loved him. Although he understood that he had sin in his life and needed Jesus, he wasn't ready to commit his life to Christ. After many conversations and much prayer, Brandon did make a decision to follow Christ. Brandon is now in the eighth grade and his relationship with Christ is growing. So much so that Brandon has begun to share his faith with his friends and has led one friend to a saving relationship with Christ! Jon explains, "We never know how God will be glorified through the ministry to which He has called each of us. He has a way of multiplying our meager efforts for eternal glory."

REAL LIFE SCENARIOS

Leading at School

Jessica loves Biology, and she especially loves it when her class has lab experiments to do. Jessica thinks she might want to be a pharmacist or a doctor someday. But Jessica is frustrated with her lab partner, Allie. Allie never participates. She sits back and waits for Jessica to do all the work. The last time Jessica and Allie worked on an experiment, it was Allie's responsibility to type up their lab results. Allie turned in the assignment more than a week late, and she and Jessica received a C minus for the project as a result. Grades are very important to Jessica because she wants to get into a good college. Jessica has decided that for the remainder of the year she is going to be responsible for all the lab reports, making sure they are done well and turned in on time. She is not going to tell Allie about her decision, but just take over all of the lab responsibilities. Allie's welcome to sit at the lab table and watch, but Jessica doesn't want her doing anything else. Is Jessica a servant leader?

Leading at Church

Amanda, the youth minister, has assigned all the youth to be on teams to plan different ministry projects for the coming year. There are five students on Kym's team, including Neil. Their team is planning a worship service for the residents at the nearby retirement center. At their first team meeting, Neil said he wanted to lead in the prayer or read the Scripture. When Neil volunteered, Kym had to force herself not to roll her eyes. Neil's nice and everything, but he stutters—and it drives Kym crazy. "Neil is the last person who should be praying or reading Scripture," Kym thought. Kym got the responsibility for writing up the assignments of each of the team members. She has decided to ignore Neil's request to pray or read Scripture. She put Neil's name down to help collect the offering. "That's a perfect job for Neil," Kym thought. Is Kym a servant leader?

Unit 9
Scripture Memorization: A Spiritual Discipline

9

Introduction
How Important Is Scripture to You?

When I was a seminary student, I had the privilege of working on staff at a missions camp for youth. During camp, we put together a simulation event that allowed students to have a taste of what it was like to live in a country hostile to Christians.

The evening began with a normal worship service. At the conclusion of worship, we were asked to lead our groups back to our Bible study room. Once there, we continued worshiping and sharing testimonies with one another. Amidst our time of worship, a man dressed in black broke into the room and abruptly ordered everyone up against the wall. The man began shouting at students and asking them why they were meeting together and what they were doing. He continued by holding up a Bible and saying, "If you think this book is so important, why don't you quote verses from it. If you can quote 25 verses, I will consider letting you go."

The outcome was usually pathetic. Students always started out boldly by quoting John 3:16. Next someone would quote a few verses of the Roman Road, but after that the process was grueling. Every once in a while there would be a student who had memorized an entire chapter in the Bible and would end up saving the group, but more times than not, the group faced the thought of execution.

If the Bible is so precious to us, why don't we take the time to hide it in our hearts? If we lived in North Korea, where possession of a Bible could mean execution, would we be more apt to memorize every scrap of Scripture we could find?

In this unit, students will be challenged to memorize Scripture. They will learn the benefits of filling their life with God's Word and learn to treasure the Book God has provided us for guidance and instruction.

Bible Study
Hiding God's Word in Your Heart

Before the Session
❏ Bring a large sword or butcher knife to the session to use as a visual. Keep the sword/knife in a case and out of sight until the appointed time in the lesson.

❏ Gather several concordances to be used during the session.

❏ Purchase temporary tattoos of hearts or smiley faces. Have several bowls of water and towels available for the students to apply the tattoos during the meeting.

❏ Gather needed supplies: index cards, markers, and bulletin board paper.

❏ Read through the lesson and be familiar with all Scriptures that will be mentioned.

During the Session
❏ Begin by asking students to think of different names they have heard used to describe the Bible. (For example: The Word of God, Scripture, the Good Book, God's Holy Word, etc.) List the students' responses on a chalkboard or large piece of bulletin board paper.

❏ Read aloud Hebrews 4:12. Bring out a knife or sword as a visual. Ask students: *Why do you think God's Word is being compared to a sword?* Explain that this lesson will focus on how Scripture gives encouragement and direction to our lives. Like a sword, it penetrates the soul and keeps us on track in our daily walk with Him.

❏ Ask for a volunteer to read 2 Timothy 3:16–17. Ask for a volunteer to point out what the verse is saying in his or her own words. Explain that these verses tell us that all Scripture comes from God. Ask students to explain why it is important for us to read the Bible and memorize Scripture.

❏ Ask for another volunteer to read Romans 15:4. Ask students: *Why was the Bible written?* Be sure to say that through Scripture we are promised to have hope in all situations.

❏ Ask students to brainstorm situations in which teenagers face difficult situations. Write the students' answers on another large sheet of paper. Divide the students into several smaller groups. Assign each group a different difficult situation. Ask the groups to use their concordances to find Scriptures that would encourage a youth facing those situations. After five minutes, have each group share the Scriptures they found. (Craig Klempnauer, "The Mighty Sword," in *StraighTrak: Teen Bible Studies on Current Issues* vol.7.)

❏ Read Psalm 119:11. Ask for a volunteer to explain the meaning of the verse. Ask students: *Why is it important for us to know what God's Word says?* Allow some time for discussion.

❏ Ask for two volunteers to come to the front of the meeting area. Tell them you are going to give them a topic, and you would like them to share all that they know about it in one minute. For the first volunteer, ask him or her to speak about something relating to politics or science. Choose a topic about which he or she will have very little knowledge. For the second volunteer, choose a subject that he or she will be able to talk about easily. This might include a sport for someone who is athletic or be about a hobby the person is interested in. After both have completed their speeches, compare the situation to us sharing Scripture. When an opportunity presents itself, would we rather stammer all over the place, or would it be better to be able to easily share God's Word?

Close the Session

❏ Give each student a temporary tattoo of a heart or smiley face. Have them put their tattoo in a place that they can see often and that will remind them to hide God's Word in their hearts this week. Have students write Psalm 119:11 on an index card. Ask students to tape the card on their bathroom mirror at home. Encourage them to memorize the card each morning as they are getting ready for school.

❏ Close the session in prayer, thanking God for His Word and asking for His help as each student commits to hiding God's Word in his or her heart this week.

Learning Activity
Making Scripture Memory Fun

Before the Session

❏ Set up three workstations with tables and chairs.

❏ Gather the following supplies and place them in the middle of each table according to the directions below.
  • **Workstation one supplies:** drawing paper, tempera paint, markers, paintbrushes, paper towels, and water cups
  • **Workstation two supplies:** magnetic strips cut in one inch pieces (found in the craft section of a department store), fine-tip permanent markers in various colors, and resealable plastic bags
  • **Workstation three supplies:** paint chips of various colors and sizes (found in the paint section of a department store), scissors, and gel pens of various colors

During the Session

❏ As students enter, have them choose one of the three workstations and be seated. Begin the lesson by asking a volunteer to read Hebrews 4:12, 2 Timothy 2:14–17, and 2 Peter 1:20–21. Explain that during this session students will be focusing on the importance of Scripture memorization. Each student will rotate through the three workstations. Each station will present a unique way to memorize Scripture. At each table, the student will make something that will help him or her memorize a particular verse. By the end of the session, students should know three new verses. Allow each student to work for 15 minutes and then rotate to the next table.

Workstation one: Choose five different verses that students can choose from to memorize. Write each verse on a piece of construction paper and tape it to the table.

Give students drawing paper and paints. Have students draw a picture that illustrates the verse. Some verses to consider: Psalm 119:11, Matthew 7:7, John 15:5, Galatians 5:22–23, Ephesians 4:29.

Workstation two: Choose a verse you would like the students to memorize. Have students use fine-tip permanent markers to write each word of the verse on individual magnetic strips. Students can decorate each strip however they like. Encourage students to put the magnets on their refrigerators in the correct order so they can work on memorizing the verse each morning at breakfast. Provide snack size zipper-lock bags for students to take their magnets home.

Workstation three: Have students choose five different paint chips. Using gel pens, have students write on each paint chip a verse they would like to memorize during the week. Encourage students to carry the paint chips in their pockets and use them for review whenever they have a few spare minutes.

Close the Session

❑ Bring the groups together and ask several volunteers to recite the Scriptures they learned during the session. Encourage students to review their verses throughout the week using the methods they learned tonight. Plan to ask the students to recite their verses at the beginning of the next session.

Ministry/Witnessing
Sharing Your Faith Without Fear

Before the Session

❑ Copy and cut the cards provided (p. 67).
❑ Cut a large sheet of paper and hang it on the wall at the front of the meeting room.
❑ Gather the following supplies: markers, index cards, and ink pens or highlighters.
❑ Make a poster board of the passages that make up the Roman Road.
❑ Purchase paperback Bibles for students to give away.

During the Session

❑ Explain to students that you are going to play a game of Taboo. Ask two people to volunteer. One volunteer will draw a card. On the card will be a word at the top that is underlined with five words listed underneath. The object is for the one who has the card to describe the underlined word to the rest of the group without using any of the words that are listed underneath. The describer will have 30 seconds to get the group to say the word. The second volunteer will serve as the judge. If the describer uses any of the words listed underneath, they will make some sort of sound to indicate that the describer made a mistake or used too much time and another volunteer will be asked to come and draw a card.

❑ Play several rounds, allowing each student a chance to describe the word.

❑ Ask students: *What makes this game hard?* Allow a few students to respond to the question. Say: *Tonight we are going to talk about sharing our faith. Just like in Taboo, when we decide we want to share our faith with a friend, we tend to talk all around the subject. It seems easier to do that than to come right out and ask our friend if he or she has a personal relationship with Jesus.*

❑ Divide the group into several smaller groups. Assign one of the following Bible passages to each group: Matthew 19:16–22; Luke 19:1–10; Luke 23:26–43; John 3:1–21; or John 4:1–26, 39. Ask each group to read the passage and find out how Jesus responded to people who were looking for direction in their lives. After five minutes, allow each group to share its thoughts about the Scripture it was assigned. Ask students: *Why did people constantly gather around Jesus? Why was it easy for some to accept Jesus while others couldn't?* Say: *Even though there were some who rejected the message Jesus preached, He continued to share the story of salvation with anyone who would listen.*

❑ Direct students' attention to the large sheet of paper on the wall. Take a few minutes to brainstorm why we don't like to witness to our friends and family. Ask students: *What are some excuses we use when it comes to witnessing?* After students have listed several excuses, ask students to list some things they could do to make witnessing easier. Explain that one way to do that is to know the Scriptures that share the gospel message.

❏ Ask students to open their Bibles to Romans for this activity. Give each student a 3-by-5 index card and an ink pen. List the following passages on the chalkboard or on poster board (If using poster board, display at the front of the room.): Romans 3:23, Romans 6:23, Romans 5:8, Romans 6:12, and Romans 6:3–5.

❏ Begin by having students turn to Romans 3:23. Read the verse, explain it, and have students use the index card to underline the verse. In the margin, next to the verse, have students write 6:23. This will help them remember to turn to Romans 6:23 next. Have students turn to Romans 6:23. Read the verse, explain it, and use the index card to underline the verse. In the margin, have students write 5:8. Turn to Romans 5:8. Read the verse, explain it, and underline the verse. In the margin, write 6:12. Turn to Romans 6:12. Read the verse, explain it, and underline the verse. In the margin write 6:3–5. Turn to the last verse, read it, and explain it to the group. Tell the students they have just read through what is known as the Roman Road. Explain to them that they have read and marked the Scriptures that support God's free gift of salvation. Explain that many missionaries use this method of marking passages in paperback Bibles to give to friends who have questions about becoming a Christian.

Close the Session

❏ Challenge each student to think about one person in her life who she would like to witness to this week. Lead the group in a time of prayer. During the prayer, leave a few moments of silence when students can pray specifically for the people God has laid on their hearts.

Cultural Experience
Blind Faith

Before the Session

❏ Invite a blind person to come and speak to your group. Ask the individual to share with the students how they read and memorize Scripture. If there is not a blind person available to speak to your group, invite a senior adult who struggles with vision problems. Another option would be to invite someone who has worked with the blind to share his or her experiences in ministering to this group.

❏ Go to your local library and check out a book that is written in Braille. If possible, get a book of the Bible that has been written in Braille. If you have trouble finding a book in Braille, check out a book written in large print.

❏ Have a blindfold for each student.

❏ Invite adult volunteers to help during this session. If possible, plan for one volunteer for every student.

During the Session

❏ As students arrive, give each a blindfold to put on. Assign an adult volunteer to each student to stay with him or her throughout the session. Have volunteers take the student by the hand and seat him or her.

❏ Tell students that for tonight's session, they will each experience what it is like to be visually impaired. For the remainder of the session, students will remain blindfolded. Tell them that they each have a volunteer who will sit with them and help them throughout the session. Allow a few minutes for each volunteer to introduce himself or herself to the student.

❏ Introduce the speaker to your students. Ask the speaker to plan a time during his or her talk to have students memorize Scripture with the help of their volunteers. The volunteer will read the Scripture to the student, while the student uses the methods the speaker suggests for memorization. Encourage the speaker to tell how he or she studies and meditates on the Bible. Allow time for students to ask questions at the end of the talk.

- After the speaker is finished, allow the students to take off their blindfolds. Ask them to describe how they felt during the activity. Ask them to think about what it would be like to be blind.
- Explain that there are many people who struggle with vision impairments. Ask students to take a few minutes to think about ways they could minister to those who cannot see clearly. Challenge students to come up with a ministry project they could do to minister to the blind.
- Some ideas to consider: (1) record Christian magazines on tape; (2) visit a nursing home and read to the senior adults who have problems with their eyesight; (3) collect old eyeglasses and send them to a ministry that will distribute them overseas.

Close the Session

- Show the group a book that is written in Braille. Explain that many people with visual impairments must read books written in Braille. Pray that God would provide the finances for those who are blind to be able to have their own Bible to read in Braille.
- Challenge students to plan a ministry project that would share the love of Christ with someone who is visually impaired.

Missionary Ministry
Pete and Janice Stanton (last frontier, Southeast Asia and Oceania)

Before the Session

- Set up your meeting room to represent an underground church. Turn all the lights off and have only one small candle burning. If possible, meet in a small room with no furniture.
- Photocopy a page of the Bible from which you will read some verses and then talk with great excitement about those verses.
- Read through the story about Pete and Janice Stanton (p. 66). Be prepared to tell the story in your own words.

During the Session

- Before the session begins, gather the students at the entrance of the meeting room. Explain to them that they will be learning about what it is like to worship in a country where being a Christian is against the law. During the session, the group will worship in an underground church setting. Tell students they will need to be silent when they enter the meeting room. If they must speak, it will need to be in a whisper. Express the urgency of the situation. Collect Bibles from the students and keep them outside of the meeting room. If students are wearing any Christian symbols, ask them to remove them before entering the room.
- As students enter, have them sit closely around the candle. Lead the worship service in a whisper. Begin by having the group sing a praise song. Everyone must whisper the words. In the middle of one of the verses, stop everyone quickly and act like you hear someone coming. Blow the candle out and listen quietly. After a minute, relight the candle and finish the song. The leader will then pull out the photocopy page of the Bible. The leader will share the Scripture with great excitement. After it is read, ask someone to share how the Scripture impacts his or her life.
- Ask someone to turn on the lights. Lead the group in a discussion about how the worship experience affected them. Explain that in many Asian countries, it is against the law to be a Christian. Those that are, risk their lives.
- Tell the story of Pete and Janice Stanton.

Close the Session

- Turn the lights off in the room and light the single candle. Ask the youth to find a place in the room where they can pray. Lead students in a guided prayertime. The leader will say a prayer request (p. 66) and allow students to pray silently for each request for 30 seconds. End the prayertime with a praise chorus.

"Pete and Janice Stanton"

Missionaries in the Pacific Rim

Pete and Janice Stanton (alias) are missionaries who serve in the Pacific Rim. The Stantons work with an unreached people group and are known as last frontier missionaries.

The Pacific Rim is in the heart of the 10/40 window. This is the region that is approximately 10 degrees to 40 degrees north of the equator that spans from North Africa to East Asia. This area contains the greatest concentration of unreached people in the world. Within this region are those who are the least evangelized due to religious persecution. For the safety of the missionaries, it is essential that their identity and location of service remain anonymous.

Although last frontier missionaries cannot share a lot about themselves or the work they are doing, they can share stories about what is happening in their ministries. This story comes directly from Janice Stanton.

"One night a neighbor of ours called out to us, 'Punden,' which means, 'Sorry. Are you there? Can I bother you?' We were at home and invited him in, only to hear a sad story. The man's wife was ill with cancer, and he wanted us to help take her to the doctor. The results were not good. The woman was in the fourth stage of breast cancer. I contacted a doctor with our organization and asked him what we could do to help the lady who I will refer to as Ibu. The doctor said to give her plenty of tender loving care. I decided to begin visiting her.

At first, it felt like my visits were futile. Ibu was very cold to my attempts to share the gospel story. I almost quit going to visit her, but then realized that as her cancer progressed, she was left alone most of the time. I saw my golden opportunity to share God's story with her. I began with the story of Adam and Eve, and then moved to Noah and the flood, then on to Abraham and his children. Finally I decided that I must tell her stories about Jesus before she died. I told Ibu a story every time I visited her. She was alone and happy to hear a story. I always asked for permission to pray with her before I went home, and she always nodded her head yes.

Finally, I got to the story of Jesus and the resurrection. I had already prayed with Ibu and was about to leave when the Spirit prompted me to ask her if she had trusted Jesus to forgive her from her sins. She smiled and gave me that slow nod of hers I was so accustomed to seeing. Ibu died a week later. Although I had a deep sense of loss, I had great hope that she had died as His child and I would see her again in eternity. I'm so thankful I didn't give up on her. I'm so glad I learned the stories that could point her to the Savior."

The Stantons use chronological Bible storying in their ministry. As you can see from Janice's story, the people are hungry to know of a loving God that cares for them.

Prayer Requests

- Pray for the Stantons and other last frontier missionaries who are serving in the 10/40 window.
- Pray for those who have accepted Jesus in these last frontier areas. Pray for their safety.
- Pray for those with whom the Stantons work every day. Pray they will have opportunities to share the gospel message.
- Praise God for the freedom you have to worship openly.

Game Cards

Witnessing
Share
Testimony
Conversation
Jesus
Faith

Jesus
Savior
Master
King
Lord
Son of God

Scripture
Bible
God's Word
Memorize
Book
Holy

Faith
Belief
See
Hope
Confidence
Promise

Excuses
Explanation
Justify
Apology
Reason
Lie

Bible
Scripture
God's Word
Holy
Jesus
Stories

Evangelism
Sharing
Telling
Bible
Testimony
Preacher

Friend
Companion
Listener
Pal
Comrade
Mate

Memorize
Remember
Practice
Recall
Think
Memory

Christianity
Religion
Jesus
Baptism
Follower
Disciple

Unit 10
We Need Each Other

Introduction
A Simple Gift of Kindness

After I finished college, I felt God calling me to serve in missions. I had the honor of serving as a US/C2 missionary for the North American Mission Board. I served in Seminole, Oklahoma, at Indian Nations Baptist Church. I didn't have a regular job at the church. I never knew from day to day what I would be doing. I loved working at the church, but there were days when it was a very lonely place to be.

My family thought I was nuts for moving ten hours away to serve in a place where I knew no one. They didn't understand why I wanted to do it, but they supported me in my decision to follow God's call.

I lived in a one-room apartment that was the size of a large closet. I will always remember the feeling I had when my parents unloaded my furniture and left. As tears were rolling down my face (as well as my mom's), I kept thinking, "What have I gotten myself into?" The two years I served were years of great spiritual growth for me. I had to depend on God to provide for me spiritually and emotionally. He provided some wonderful people who took care of me during those two years, but they never took the place of my family.

I would feel particularly alone during the holidays. There is never a substitute for being with the ones you love during that time of year. One particular year, the church decided to purchase poinsettias in memory of people who had passed away or in honor of others that were special to the church family. It was my job to set up the project. After I collected the money to purchase the plants, I went to the local florist and told them I wanted to purchase poinsettias for our church. As I was

explaining who I was and what I wanted to purchase, I realized that there was another lady in the store who was purchasing poinsettias. The poinsettias she bought were huge plants covered with beautiful, large, red flowers. The plants I was buying were a bit smaller. As I was loading my car with the plants I purchased, the lady came up to me and gave me one of the huge poinsettia plants. She said she wanted me to have one and then wished me a Merry Christmas.

I never knew the woman's name or who she was, but to this day I believe she was an angel who was put there to minister to me during a time when I needed it most.

This unit focuses on the importance of building up one another through encouragement, kindness, and compassion. Students will be challenged to evaluate those people in their lives who need to be shown God's love through a simple act of kindness. May we all take time to encourage those around us in Christ's name.

Bible Study
One Body

Before the Session
❏ Bring a ball of yarn to use during this session.
❏ Read through the Scripture and become familiar with the lesson.

During the Session
❏ Explain that students will have to work together as a team to accomplish this activity. Begin by having students stand shoulder to shoulder in a circle and hold hands. Assign each student a number. Tell students that when you say go, those who have an odd number

will lean back, and at the same time, those who have an even number will lean forward. Students will need to keep their bodies stiff and knees locked as they lean forward or back. If done correctly, the end result will produce a star-like formation with the weight of each person balancing the other.

❏ Ask students the following questions to promote discussion:
  • *Was this a hard activity to accomplish? If so, why?*
  • *What would have made it easier?*
  • *What makes this activity work?*
  • *What about our Youth on Mission℠ group, how does it function? How would you describe our group to someone who has never been to a meeting?*

❏ Say: *Today we will focus on affirming one another in who we are as individuals and who we are as a group.* Divide the students into two groups. Have one group read 1 Corinthians 12:12–25. Assign the other group to read Ephesians 4:29–32. Give each group one of the following tasks to perform after students have read their passages.

  Group 1 (1 Corinthians)—Think about the members of our youth group, assign each person a body part that would best represent his or her personality. Be ready to share your answers with the entire group. (Ex. Sarah would be an ear, because she is a great listener.)

  Group 2 (Ephesians)—Prepare a short drama that illustrates the passage. Include each person of the group in the drama.

❏ Allow groups 10 minutes to prepare their presentations. Have each group share its Scripture and presentation with the large group.

Close the Session

❏ Have students sit in a circle. Explain that you are going to end the meeting with a web of affirmation. Give one student a ball of yarn. Have them hold on to the end of the yarn and throw the other end to someone in the group. Tell them to say an encouraging word about the person they threw the ball to. That person will hold the string and throw the yarn to someone else. Continue the same process until every member of the group has been affirmed and is holding the string.

❏ End the session by leading the group in prayer. Pray for unity among the members of the group.

Learning Activity
Ministry of Kindness

Before the Session

❏ Copy and then cut apart each quote on "Inspirational Quotes" (p. 72).

❏ Tape each strip of paper to a small piece of candy.

❏ Tape a large sheet of paper to the front of the meeting area. Have a marker available.

❏ Read through the ideas of encouragement in During the Session. Gather the needed supplies to perform one or more of the activities during the session.

During the Session

❏ As students enter, give each a piece of candy with a kindness quote taped to it. Ask students to read the quotes aloud. Explain that during this session, they will focus on showing kindness to people in their church. Ask students to share an experience they have had when kindness was shown to them or when they did something kind for someone else. Ask students: *How did it make you feel to do a kind act for someone? How did it feel when someone did something nice for you?*

❏ Ask students to identify people in the church who need encouragement. Direct students to think about people who rarely receive recognition for the work they do. Write the names of each individual on a large piece of paper.

❏ Ask the students to identify one person on the list they would like to encourage as a group. Plan an activity to do during the session that shows love and kindness to that person. See page 71 for ideas.

After the Session

❏ Allow each student to choose one of the names written on the poster at the beginning of the session. Challenge students to anonymously perform a random act of kindness for that person before your next meeting.

Encouragement Ideas

• Fork your youth pastor's yard! Buy a pack of plastic forks and construction paper. Have students cut out different shapes from the paper and write an affirmation for the person on each shape. Tape the construction paper to the handle of the fork using heavy tape. If possible, go at night and stick the forks in the yard. In the morning your youth pastor will be pleasantly surprised to open his or her door to a lawn full of encouraging notes! (Heather Rabbon, "Twist on Lawn Forking," Egad! Ideas, www.egadideas.com/ideas.asp.)

• Collect a bouquet of wildflowers and put them in a glass vase. Set the vase on the front porch of the person who needs to be encouraged. Ring the doorbell and run!

• Deliver a small pizza to a youth who is experiencing some difficulties in his or her life.

• Decorate your pastor's office with balloons that have encouraging notes written on them.

• Deliver a box of chocolates or a bag of candy to a senior adult who has a servant heart.

Ministry/Witnessing
To the Community with Love

Before the Session
❏ Plan to do this ministry project on the weekend. Ask each student to bring $5 to defray the cost of the event.
❏ Write the following phrases on slips of paper: *park, parking lot, nursing home, mall, coin laundry center, grocery store.*
❏ Fold the slips of paper in half and place them in a hat or bowl.
❏ Enlist adult volunteers to help with the project. You will need one driver per each group of four.
❏ Enlist adult volunteers to provide lunch or snacks for the groups when they return from the ministry event.

Random Acts of Kindness Ideas

Park
• Hand out balloons to children
• Give out bottled water to joggers
• Pick up trash
• Blow bubbles and give out bubbles to children

Parking lot
• Wash car windows (ask store manager for permission first)
• Put a daisy under the windshield wiper of parked cars with a card attached that reads, *Rejoice*
• Hold a free car wash
• Pick up trash

Nursing home
• Read the Bible to residents
• Decorate a meeting room with balloons and serve birthday cake
• Paint women's fingernails
• Give out flowers

Mall
• Give out balloons to children (ask mall manager for permission)
• Give a canned soda to shoppers
• Buy cookies and give them to mall employees
• Do face painting for children
• Give out free movie tickets

Coin laundry center
• Give out quarters to patrons
• Buy individual sized laundry soap and give away
• Give away packages of chips or crackers
• Give away coloring books and crayons to children
• Buy magazines to distribute

Grocery store
• Offer to gather grocery carts and return them to the store
• Carry someone's groceries to their car
• Give out balloons to children
• Give quarters to children to get bubblegum out of the gumball machine (with parent's permission)
• Give a treat to the cashier

Inspirational Quotes

"Compassion to others begins with kindness to ourselves." Pema Chodron

"Kindness is a language that the deaf can hear and the blind can read." Mark Twain

"It is well to give when asked, but it is better to give unasked, through understanding." Kahlil Gilbran

"The fragrance always stays in the hand that gives the rose." Hadia Bejar

"Do good and care not to whom." Italian proverb

"It is difficult to give away kindness. It keeps coming back to you." Cort Flint

"A candle uses none of its light by lighting another candle." Unknown

"Don't wait for people to be friendly, show them how." Unknown

"How beautiful a day can be when kindness touches it." George Alliston

"Today make an investment in someone else's happiness." Unknown

"If you can't feed a hundred people, then feed just one." Mother Teresa

"Kind words do not cost much, yet they accomplish much." Blaise Pascal

"We make a living by what we get. We make a life by what we give." Winston Churchill

"No act of kindness, however small, is ever wasted." Aesop

"Kind words can be short and easy to speak, but their echoes are truly endless." Mother Teresa

The Random Acts of Kindness Foundation, "Inspirational Quotes," http://www.actsofkindness.org/inspiration/quotes.asp

During the Session

❏ Divide the youth into groups of no more than four. Assign each group an adult volunteer to drive. Explain to each group that they are going to take part in Random Act of Kindness Day for your community.

❏ Someone from each group will draw a slip of paper out of the hat. Whatever the paper says will indicate the location where that group will go and perform a random act of kindness. Students must decide, as a group, what they will do at their location (see "Random Acts of Kindness Ideas," p. 71). They will pool their money together to buy any needed supplies. Allow each team two to three hours to accomplish its deeds.

After the Session

❏ After the designated time period, have the groups meet together for lunch or snacks. Allow students to share stories of what happened during the ministry project. Ask students to talk about how people reacted to their gifts of service.

Cultural Experience
Sharing Kindness Around the Community

Before the Session

❏ Contact your town mayor's office and ask for ideas about how your group can be of assistance to the community. Explain that your group has been focusing on serving in the church and community and would like to perform a community service project.

❏ Invite the mayor or other city representative to speak to the group about the community and how the group could minister to the community.

❏ Decide on a date and time when the group will perform the service project. Publicize the event with the students.

❏ Assist groups as needed.

During the Session

❏ Begin by introducing the city official as the guest speaker for the evening. Allow students to ask questions after the presentation.

❏ Lead the students in a time of brainstorming community service projects they can do. Make sure students take into account the suggestions of the city official. Have students vote on the ideas that were presented and settle on one option. Divide students into small groups to do the background work that will need to be completed before the project. Consider delegating students to the following groups (and assign other groups as needed):

• supplies (determining supplies that are needed, buying or having supplies donated, and making sure the supplies get to the site)

• logistics (location of the event, securing permission, promoting the event, and set-up)

• volunteers (secure adult volunteers to help with the event)

• schedule (determining what will happen at the event and who is in charge of each aspect of the project)

Community Events to Consider

• Christ Follower 5K Run/Walk
• Beautification of a City Park
• Working on a Habitat House
• International Day in the Park
• Highway Trash Pickup
• Graffiti Cleanup/Painting
• Children's Fair
• Movie Night in the Park
• Community Craft Fair Featuring International Crafts
• End of the School Year Cleanup

After the Session

❏ Allow students several weeks to work on their assignments and prepare for the event. Allow students to do the majority of the planning of the event.

Missionary Ministry
Ginger Smith (Houston, Texas)

Before the Session

❏ Contact your state WMU® office and ask if there is a Christian Women's Job Corps® (CWJC℠) site near you. If so, invite a speaker from the program to share with your students about how the program has changed her life. If there is not a CWJC nearby, request a phone number where you can call and interview someone who is part of the program. Set up a time when the group can do a phone interview during the session. Write out the questions you will ask during the phone interview. Make sure you have a speakerphone available for the session.

❏ Visit the WMU Web site www.wmu.com/getinvolved/ministry/cwjc/ to find out more facts about CWJC.

❏ Gather needed supplies: construction paper, pencils, scissors, and masking tape.

❏ Read through the story of Ginger Smith (p. 74). Be prepared to tell the story in your own words.

During the Session

❏ Begin the session by telling the story of Ginger Smith.

❏ After sharing Ginger's story, introduce your speaker for the evening. If you have set up a phone interview, designate one person who will ask the questions. Allow a few minutes at the end for students to ask questions.

Close the Session

❏ Give each student a piece of construction paper, a pencil, and a pair of scissors. Have students trace their handprint on the paper and cut it out. On the print, have them write the name of someone they know who could use a helping hand. Allow a few moments of silence when students can pray for the people they wrote down on their hands. Encourage students to do something nice for those people during the week to show them they care about them. Tape the handprints on the wall as a reminder of the session.

Ginger Smith
Houston, Texas

Ginger Smith is a missionary who serves as the administrator of the Baptist Mission Centers of Houston, Texas. The ministry was started to partner with Houston churches to help transform broken and neglected communities in the Houston area. It does this by providing for the spiritual and physical needs of people. Some of its ministries include food and clothing distribution, kids' club, preteen and teen clubs, senior adult ministries, English as a second language classes, and Christian Women's Job Corps (CWJC).

CWJC is a ministry that provides women in need a hand up toward sustaining successful employment and meeting their life goals. The program meets four days a week for ten weeks. Students are assigned a mentor who will encourage them while they are in the program. The mentor continues to be there for the student after she graduates from the program.

Through the CWJC program, women receive training in life skills and job readiness. They enter the program with four goals: (1) to begin and/or grow in a personal relationship with Jesus Christ; (2) to complete a job readiness and life skills program; (3) to fulfill the CWJC purpose; (4) to give back to the CWJC program. The CWJC purpose (to equip women for life and employment) is fulfilled when a woman has basic life skills necessary for self-sufficiency within her culture, which may include: sustained employment, adequate income, housing, transportation, child care, and/or medical care.

Ginger serves on the advisory council for CWJC and gives encouragement to the women throughout the program. In 2002, all but one of the women who participated in the program graduated. In 2003, all of the women in the program graduated! Among them was Dora Hernandez who later went on to gain her US citizenship. Dora is now on staff at the Fletcher Center as assistant director and also serves as a mentor to other women who need a helping hand.

11

Unit 11
Accountability: Who Needs It?

Introduction
Who Holds You Accountable?

My husband and I have been on a diet for what seems like forever. After we married, we realized our dating habits had caused us to put on a few unwanted pounds. We decided we would begin a healthful eating plan and hold each other accountable for what we ate each day.

The plan worked great for me. Being a newlywed, I didn't want to let my husband down. Of course he would never get mad if I slipped up and ate a piece of chocolate, but just knowing he was going to ask me how I did that day made me stick to the diet. I knew I would have to answer him truthfully. When I had tried dieting before, there was no one who asked me what I ate. If I wanted to cheat, I usually did. But now, there was someone who encouraged me to stick to the plan. He held me accountable.

There are many areas in our lives where we need accountability. As Christians, we all need to be encouraged to stay on the right track. It is so easy to be tempted to do what we know is wrong. We either figure no one will notice, or worse, no one will care.

This unit will introduce the idea of accountability groups. Students will learn the importance of being accountable to God and to one another as Christians.

Bible Study
Hold Yourself Accountable to Others

Before the Session
❏ Gather needed supplies: one pack of index cards, a roll of masking tape, and scrap paper for each group of four; blank copy paper; and pens or markers.
❏ Record a popular team sport on TV. If possible, include a segment when the team scored points in the game.
❏ Review the Scripture that will be discussed. Read through the lesson and become familiar with the activities and Scripture.
❏ Purchase a small prize for the winning team.

During the Session
❏ Divide students into groups of four. Give each group a pack of index cards, scrap paper, and a roll of masking tape. Instruct each group to use the items to make the tallest freestanding structure it can. Students can only use the three items provided. They will have ten minutes to make their structure.
❏ Determine which group's structure is the tallest and award the group a small prize. Ask students: *Why was this activity challenging? Did you work as a team or did each person have his or her own job? If you had the chance to do it again, what would you do differently? What can we learn from this activity?*
❏ Show a few minutes of a taped team-sporting event. If possible, show a portion of the game where the team scores. Ask students: *What makes a team work?* Lead in a discussion about the importance of working together and everyone doing his or her job in order to accomplish the end result.

- Say: *As Christians, we are a team. We are called to work together. As you worked together in teams, you each had certain jobs you were given. It took each of you working together to make the structure stand! As we watched the athletes play, they couldn't win the game on their own. They worked together. We each have different jobs, but we all have to contribute to complete the task. Just like the athletes, we must depend on one another for encouragement and accountability in our Christian walk.*

- Assign each group one of the following passages: John 17:20–23, Ephesians 4:3–5, and Romans 15:5–6. Have each group read its passage and come up with a one-word theme that would summarize the entire passage. Each group will then come up with a short skit or pantomime to illustrate the theme through a real-life situation. Allow each group ten minutes for this activity. Bring all the groups back together to share their verses and skits with the larger group.

Close the Session

- Tape a piece of copy paper on the back of each student. Tell students they are going to spend a few minutes affirming one another. Have students write a word of encouragement on the back of each student. Ask students to point out the qualities of each person that allows the group to function as a unified body. Close the session in prayer.

Learning Activity
Designing an Accountability Plan

Before the Session

- Gather small, cube-shaped empty tissue boxes. You will need one tissue box for every two students.

- In each box, place the following items: two chenille sticks twisted together, a key, a red heart cut out of construction paper, two pieces of candy taped together, an adhesive bandage, a nail, a rubber band, a battery, and a photocopy of the question sheet on page 77.

- Bring an egg timer to the session to limit the time spent on each question.

- Post a sign-up sheet for students to sign if they would like to participate in an accountability group on a permanent basis.

During the Session

- Explain to students that you will be starting an accountability plan for those interested in participating. Explain that an accountability plan is for people who desire a deeper relationship with Christ and want to have someone to hold them to their commitment to become a devoted Christ follower.

- Clarify that during today's session, everyone will participate in an accountability session. Have students choose a partner of the same gender for the activity. Each pair will find a place in the room where they can talk. Give each pair a tissue box filled with the items listed in Before the Session. Instruct that during an accountability meeting, the two partners discuss each other's lives and spend time in prayer for each other. Explain that you have provided the questions in the box for the students to discuss. Ask students to draw out each item one at a time. Each item represents a certain question. When they draw out an item, they will refer to the question sheet, and each person will answer the question. Students will have five minutes for each question. Use an egg timer to keep students moving through each question.

After the Session

- After students have answered all of the questions, ask each pair to spend five minutes in prayer.

- To close the meeting, have students sign up for accountability groups if they would like to meet on a consistent basis with a partner to discuss their walk with Christ. Assign groups of two or three to become accountability groups. Plan for groups to meet for 20 minutes before or after your Youth on Mission℠ meetings.

Question Sheet

Two chenille sticks —Make something out of the sticks that represents your personality.

Explain why you chose to make that particular object.

Key —What key role do you play in your family structure?

Red heart —What are you passionate about?

Two pieces of candy —What is going on in your life that makes you smile?

Adhesive bandage —What is going on in your life that makes you hurt?

Nail —How is your relationship with Christ right now?

What do you need to do to make it stronger?

Rubber band —How is God stretching you right now? What are you learning from it?

A battery —What motivates you to keep going in your Christian walk?

Question Sheet

Two chenille sticks —Make something out of the sticks that represents your personality.

Explain why you chose to make that particular object.

Key —What key role do you play in your family structure?

Red heart —What are you passionate about?

Two pieces of candy —What is going on in your life that makes you smile?

Adhesive bandage —What is going on in your life that makes you hurt?

Nail —How is your relationship with Christ right now?

What do you need to do to make it stronger?

Rubber band —How is God stretching you right now? What are you learning from it?

A battery —What motivates you to keep going in your Christian walk?

Ministry/Witnessing
Showing God's Love to Senior Adults

Before the Session

❑ Contact a local assisted living facility or nursing home and set up a time when your Youth on Mission group can host a fellowship for the residents.

❑ Consult with the director about the menu for the fellowship. Make sure the director approves the desserts you plan to serve.

❑ Ask for volunteers in the church to prepare different desserts to donate for the fellowship. Be sure to include sugar-free desserts on the menu.

❑ Ask adult volunteers to assist with the fellowship and driving.

❑ Purchase any needed supplies for the fellowship (decorations, plates, cups, plastic forks, plastic spoons, napkins, etc.).

❑ Purchase several items that can be given away as door prizes during the fellowship. (For example: a potted plant, lotion, socks, candy, a nice pen, etc.)

❑ Purchase a thank-you card and two pieces of poster board.

❑ Bring a CD player and swing music.

During the Session

❑ Students will plan a fellowship for a local nursing home or assisted living facility. Plan a time for students to put on a variety show for seniors. Have students plan a 30-minute show of music, puppets, drama, solos, dance, magic, etc. As you plan, take into account the talents of each of the students who will participate. Use this opportunity to encourage those students who may not be the first to volunteer to share their talents, to do so during this activity.

❑ Invite a student to tell a story and lead in a devotion time. If you don't have a student who could lead in this activity, invite a pastor or minister to lead in this portion of the fellowship.

Tentative Schedule for the Event

Greetings and Music—As residents enter, have students greet them and give them name tags. Have lively swing music playing in the background. Have students escort residents to a table.

Coffee and Desserts—Have students prepare a menu that lists the different desserts that are available. Have students take orders from residents and serve them their choice of dessert and coffee.

Entertainment—Designate an MC for the evening. This person should be prepared to tell a few jokes and introduce the different acts throughout the evening.

Speaker—After the entertainment, the MC will introduce the speaker. The speaker will finish the evening with a story and devotion.

Door Prizes—The MC will give away several door prizes at the end of the evening.

Good-byes and Cleanup—Have students help residents return to their rooms. Make sure the meeting room is in the same order as when you arrived.

After the Session

❑ Have students write a thank-you note to the facility director. Have students make a poster-sized thank-you to send to the residents for allowing the group to come.

❑ Deliver the cards to the facility.

Cultural Experience
Share Your Thoughts

Before the Session

❑ Invite six adults to come and participate in a panel discussion. If possible, include a person from each of the following categories: a new Christian, a senior adult, a Sunday School teacher, a college student, and a young couple who has children. Tell each guest he or she will be participating in a panel discussion about the importance of Christian fellowship and accountability in his or her spiritual walk.

❑ Prepare several questions to ask the panel. Consider some of the following:

• *What do you do in your daily routine to keep your relationship with God strong?*

• *Who holds you accountable in being a faithful witness?*

• *Why is it important for you to be involved actively in a church?*

• *Do you ever struggle in your Christian walk? If so, how do you overcome that feeling?*

• *What is your advice to a teenager about staying grounded in his or her relationship with Christ?*

❑ Set up six chairs in a row at the front of the room.

❑ Gather needed supplies: paper and pencils.

❑ Plan to serve light refreshments after the panel discussion.

During the Session

❑ As students arrive, explain that during this session they will have the opportunity to interview some adults about their Christian walk and the importance of fellowship with other believers and accountability to one another in their spiritual walk. Allow panelists to introduce themselves. Have them tell a little bit about who they are and how long they have been at the church.

❑ Give each student a piece of paper and pen. Ask students to write down three questions they would like to ask the panel. Make sure students understand the topic you will be discussing before they write down their questions.

❑ After students write their questions, choose several questions for each panel participant to answer. If necessary, use some of the questions you prepared before the session.

Close the Session

❑ Ask the entire group to divide into two smaller groups of men and women. Have each group spend a few minutes sharing prayer requests, and then ask a panelist to lead the group in prayer.

❑ Provide refreshments and allow time for panelists and youth to mingle, and ask more questions if needed.

Missionary Ministry
Jeff Whitfield (Republic of Ireland)

Before the Session

❑ Read through the story of Jeff Whitfield (p. 80). Be prepared to tell his story in your own words.

❑ Arrange for three youth to read an Irish blessing at the beginning of the session (p. 81).

❑ Check out a CD of Irish music from your local library. Make sure you have a CD player available for the session.

❑ Gather paper and pens for students to use at the end of the session.

❑ Bring a globe or world map to the session. Locate Ireland and mark it with a green shamrock.

❑ Write out the following prayer requests on green shamrock shapes cut out of construction paper:

• *Pray for Jeff Whitfield and his family as they serve other missionaries through counseling and pastoral care.*

• *Pray for the church Jeff is helping to start.*

• *Pray the new believers will learn what it means to be peacemakers.*

• *Pray for local believers to share the gospel story with their friends and family.*

• *Pray for other missionaries in the region who serve under tight security.*

• *Pray for Jeff as he travels to different areas in the region to meet with missionaries.*

During the Session

❏ Begin the session with the reading of three Irish blessings. Have the assigned students come to the front of the room and read their blessings. When they are finished, tell the story of Jeff Whitfield.

❏ Ask students: *Do any of you know what you just heard?* Explain that students just heard three Irish blessings. Say: *The missionary we will be studying today serves in the Republic of Ireland.* (Use this opportunity to show students where Ireland is located on a map or globe.)

❏ Ask students the following questions to generate discussion about the story:

• *If your job was to provide pastoral care for missionaries, what would you do to minister to them?*

• *Why is it important for Jeff to establish accountability groups among the Irish people?*

❏ Say: *At the beginning of the session, you heard three Irish blessings. Take a few minutes to write your own blessing for the group.*

❏ Allow students ten minutes to write an Irish blessing for the group. Play Irish music while students are working. Allow students to work in groups for this activity.

After the Session

❏ Allow students to read their Irish blessings to the group. Close the session by giving each student a shamrock with a prayer request taped on it. Explain to students that it is said that St. Patrick used the shamrock to explain the concept of the trinity, which refers to the Father, the Son, and the Holy Spirit. This explains the association of the shamrock with St. Patrick's Day. Ask one student to lead the group in a closing prayer for Jeff Whitfield and the work he does in Ireland.

Jeff Whitfield
Western Europe

Jeff Whitfield is a missionary who serves as a pastoral care consultant for the Western Europe Region. Jeff provides pastoral care to the missionaries in the region.

Jeff and his family live in the Republic of Ireland. They work in church planting efforts with a local church that has about 30 members. Many of these individuals were saved as adults and come from a traditional Irish Catholic background. Jeff says 90 percent of the Irish population claims the Catholic religion, yet only 1 percent claims a saving relationship with Jesus Christ.

Jeff describes the Irish people as "typically friendly on a surface level, but deeply engrained in the national psyche is a general mistrust of others due to a long history of being under the domain of another nation against their will. In order for more people to come to Christ and new churches to be planted, the believers must learn to live at peace, to forgive, and to be reconciled with one another in the same way that God forgave them and reconciled them to Himself through Christ."

One way Jeff teaches a lifestyle of love and peace is through teaching discipleship courses. He is currently teaching a discipleship series titled Biblical Peacemaking with 25 local believers. "These discipleship groups are focused on obedience-based discipleship that utilizes the Bible, workbooks, homework, and weekly teaching and discipleship groups." Jeff emphasizes the need for students to hold one another accountable during the study. He wants the believers to learn the importance of community and fellowship in the Christian life.

Jeff is always looking for new ways to reach those seeking something more in life. He has established explorer groups that invite the people from the neighborhoods to gather at someone's home weekly for six to ten weeks to study about who Christ is and what it means to be a Christian. It is through these groups that Jeff hopes to cultivate relationships among the Irish people in order to gain their trust and be able to share the gospel with them.

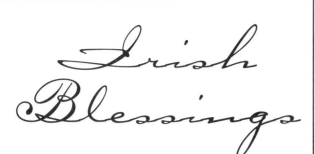

Irish Blessings

Give us, Lord, a bit o sun,

A bit o work and a bit o fun,

Give us in all the struggle and sputter,

Our daily bread and a bit o butter.

Give us health our keep to make

And a bit to spare for other's sake.

Give us, too, a bit of song

And a tale and a book to help us along.

Give us, Lord, a chance to be

Our goodly best, brave, wise and free,

Our goodly best for ourselves and others

Till all men learn to live as brothers.

May God guard you

through each night and day

and ever watch above you.

May God smile on all you do

and always, may God love you!

May God give you . . .

For every storm, a rainbow,

For every tear, a smile,

For every care, a promise,

And a blessing in each trial.

For every problem life sends,

A faithful friend to share,

For every sigh, a sweet song,

And an answer for each prayer.

Irish Culture and Customs, "Blessings,"
www.irishcultureandcustoms.com/Blessings/Bless.html.

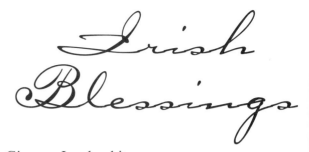

Irish Blessings

Give us, Lord, a bit o sun,

A bit o work and a bit o fun,

Give us in all the struggle and sputter,

Our daily bread and a bit o butter.

Give us health our keep to make

And a bit to spare for other's sake.

Give us, too, a bit of song

And a tale and a book to help us along.

Give us, Lord, a chance to be

Our goodly best, brave, wise and free,

Our goodly best for ourselves and others

Till all men learn to live as brothers.

May God guard you

through each night and day

and ever watch above you.

May God smile on all you do

and always, may God love you!

May God give you . . .

For every storm, a rainbow,

For every tear, a smile,

For every care, a promise,

And a blessing in each trial.

For every problem life sends,

A faithful friend to share,

For every sigh, a sweet song,

And an answer for each prayer.

Irish Culture and Customs, "Blessings,"
www.irishcultureandcustoms.com/Blessings/Bless.html.

Unit 12
Becoming Christ Followers Through Unity

Introduction
Unity

Adventure recreation uses an element of risk and excitement to build unity within a group. Those who participate in the activities build trust through games and rope courses. It is through these activities that participants discover spiritual truths.

I have always been a fan of adventure recreation games, but I never wanted to participate in them. It is the risk part that keeps me from being openly cooperative. You see, I am a chicken when it comes to taking risks. I like being safe. My philosophy is, why put yourself in danger when you don't have to?

Several years ago, during a camp staff training event, I was encouraged to participate in a ropes course. There was no way out of the situation. If I didn't do it, I would look like a coward in front of my co-workers. The best thing I could do was pray for courage and hope for the best!

The ropes element we were doing required my partner and I to climb a tree and basically walk a tightrope across a wire the size of a shoelace. There were some other elements involved, but you get the picture. I was petrified. Not being the most athletic person in the world, it was a struggle just to climb the tree. I managed to make it to the top in a respectable amount of time, but then the tightrope walking began. Have you ever walked on something the size of a shoelace? It is difficult.

I took one step, while holding on to a guide wire overhead, and my knees started shaking. I knew I had to try, but I was scared. It was at that moment I began to realize what was going on below me. My co-workers were saying, "Way to go! You're doing great! You can do it! Don't look down!" My friends were cheering me on. They knew I was petrified, so they encouraged me to keep going.

When I returned safely to the ground, I was so proud of myself. I had conquered a fear, but more than that, I had formed a bond with my co-workers. It was their encouragement that got me through the ordeal.

We all need encouragement in our daily walk as Christ followers. God never intended for us to do it alone. This unit will focus on group unity. Your group will participate in activities that will strengthen them as individuals as well as a group.

Bible Study
All a Part of the Body

Before the Session

❏ You will need an inexpensive gift for each student. Wrap the gifts in individual boxes and display them on a table as students enter. Some gifts to consider: loose change, toilet paper, candy, a picture of a smile, a pack of gum, a dollar bill, etc.

❏ Gather needed supplies: CD player, markers, 4 large boxes the groups can wrap, wrapping paper, scissors, ribbon, construction paper and tape for each group to wrap their box, a large beautifully wrapped box with miniature Christmas ornaments in the shape of a gift inside—one for each student, or a ribbon for each student with a small cross attached, pens for each student, small pieces of construction paper—one per student, white stick-on labels.

❏ A copy of the song, "If We Are the Body" by Casting Crowns.

❏ Read through the entire lesson and determine if the activities are appropriate for your group.

❏ Review the Scriptures. Be prepared to answer questions about spiritual gifts.

❑ Gather several Bible resources, such as Bible dictionaries and Bible encyclopedias, to be used during the session.

❑ Write each of the following on a gift tag, Christmas card, or birthday party invitation:

• *What was the best gift you ever received? Why?*

• *Do you still have that gift somewhere at home?*

• *What is the best gift you have ever given and to whom did you give it?*

• *What did the person do when they received this special gift from you?*

During the Session

❑ As students arrive, divide them into groups of three or four and discuss the following questions printed on gift tags, Christmas cards, or birthday party invitations:

• *What was the best gift you ever received? Why?*

• *Do you still have that gift somewhere at home?*

• *What is the best gift you have ever given and to whom did you give it?*

• *What did the person do when they received this special gift from you?*

❑ Allow the groups of students time to share their answers with one another. Then ask the students to form a large group and allow some of those present to share their answers to the above questions with everyone. Ask, *Why do we love to receive gifts so much? How does it make us feel to receive a gift? What can we know about a person who gives us a special gift?*

❑ Tell the students that you have brought gifts for each of them. Allow the students to go the table prepared with all of the gifts. Guide the students to open their gifts and then answer the following questions: *Do you like the gift you received? Why or why not? Would you like to share your gift with others in the room? Why or why not?*

❑ Bring out the large, beautifully wrapped gift that you prepared ahead of time. Ask someone to come to the front and open the gift in front of the rest of the group. Tell the student that the gift is only for him, and as he opens it, he cannot show it to anyone else, or tell anyone else what is inside.

❑ When the volunteer has opened the gift and taken the closed box back to her seat, ask the group: *How does it feel to not know what is in the box that _____ (student's name) opened? How do you feel when someone shares a gift with you? How does it feel when someone keeps a gift only to herself?*

❑ Say, *God has given each of us gifts that He wants us to use and share with others. Do any of you know what some of your God-given gifts are? Well, we all have God-given gifts, even if sometimes we don't feel very gifted. So that's what we're going to look at today.*

❑ Divide the large group into four smaller groups. Provide each small group with a box, wrapping paper, ribbons, scissors, and tape. Ask the groups to work together to wrap their gifts as beautifully as they can.

❑ Once the gifts have been wrapped. Provide each group with one of the following passages of Scripture to read: Romans 12:38 or 1 Corinthians 12:431. Give each group a set of markers and some white stick-on labels. Guide the groups use their markers to list different gifts they saw in their passage that God gives to us, one per label. Instruct the groups to stick the labels all over the outside of their gifts. Groups can use Bible dictionaries or a spiritual gifts Web site to look up definitions of each spiritual gift, which they can also write on the labels indicating each gift.

❑ Bring the large group back together and ask two individuals to read aloud each of the passages. Ask the group, *Now that you've read these passages, what do you think a spiritual gift is? Do you believe everyone has a spiritual gift? Does God give everyone spiritual gifts? Why or why not? What should we do with the spiritual gifts God gives us?*

❑ Ask each group to share what they have learned. If you have multiple groups who have studied the same passage, allow each group to share several gifts they learned about in their passage. Unlike the beautiful gift that _____ (student's name) opened earlier, God intends us to share our spiritual gifts with others. Allow the student who opened the special gift to share the contents with everyone in the group—possibly miniature Christmas ornaments shaped like gifts or a piece of ribbon for everyone in the group with a cross ornament hung on one end. Tell the students that these are to remind them of the spiritual gifts God has given them, and that they are to use them for the benefit of others.

❏ Ask the students to spread out in the room and give each individual a pen and a small piece of construction paper. Ask the students to look at the spiritual gifts they have studied, listed on the outside of the wrapped packages, and write on their paper the gift(s) they believe God has given them. Remind them that every child of God has been given a spiritual gift.

Close the Session

❏ Ask the students to remain in their seats throughout the room and reflect for a few minutes on what they have learned. Play the song, "If We Are the Body? by Casting Crowns. After the song, ask the students to reflect on their church. Have them grade the church on unity. Ask them to think of some ideas about how the group could promote unity among the church body. Plan to implement one of the ideas within the next month.

❏ Pray to close the meeting.

Learning Activity
Strengthening the Group

Before the Session

❏ For this retreat, you will need to create the atmosphere of the popular show, *Survivor.* Plan to hold the retreat at a campground or in a neighborhood where two houses are close together.

❏ Ask for two tents to be donated for the retreat.

❏ Purchase the needed food supplies for the weekend. Try to keep food to a minimum. Serve natural foods such as fruit, bread, rice, beans, etc.

❏ Set up the challenges as described in the lesson.

❏ Purchase a bandana for each student. The bandanas will need to be two different colors to represent two different teams.

❏ Purchase two standard pillowcases. Provide paint and brushes for each team to decorate a pillowcase.

❏ Purchase two lengths of rope 40 to 80 feet long.

❏ Plan a work ministry project that the students will participate in on Saturday morning.

❏ Obtain a hat.

❏ Cut some paper into small squares—one square for each student. Write the number 1 on half of all the squares and the number 2 on the other half.

During the Session

❏ As students arrive, have them put all of their belongings in a certain place. Divide the group into two equal groups by having students draw a number out of a hat. All the number ones will get one bandana color while all the number twos will get the other. Give students a few minutes to think of a name for their "tribe." Give each group a pillowcase to decorate to represent its tribe's flag.

❏ Tell students they will not be taking any of their belongings with them. Give them three minutes to choose one item that will be their luxury item that they may bring along. Have an adult pack up the rest of the luggage and bring it to be used as a reward in one of the challenges.

❏ Drive the students to their designated tribe locations. Give them a tent to set up for their first task. Tell the students that both groups will meet at a designated place and time to participate in their first challenge.

❏ **Challenge One:**
Set up a race that the students must maneuver through. The race will consist of four stops along the way. Each stop should be well marked. The point of the race is for students to recount the lessons of the year. Tie students' arms together with their bandanas. They will have to move together as a team to complete the activity at each stop. The first team to the finish line will win a reward. The reward will be their pillows, blankets, and air mattresses.

Stop One—Each person must eat something disgusting. Ex. pickled egg, ripe banana, smoked fish, etc. The group cannot move to the next station until everyone has eaten the item.

Stop Two—The group must decide on a worship chorus and sing one verse and chorus.

Stop Three—The group will play a game of Pictionary. Give each group five words that five members of the team must draw and the rest of the team must guess. Once all five words have been successfully guessed, the group may move on. The words to be drawn are: Bible, Scripture memory, worship, Christ follower, and servant heart.

Stop Four—The group will form a tight circle and be bound together by a rope (an adult volunteer will need to do this). The group, as a whole, will have to walk to the finish line.

❑ After the challenge, the groups will return to their tribes and eat dinner and have a devotion time. Invite several college students or adults to go to the tribe and share their testimony with the group. Ask the special guests to talk about the importance of unity and how it affects our witness for Christ.

❑ **Challenge Two:**

Each tribe will be given a rope that is 40 to 80 feet in length. (The length is dependant on how many people are in each tribe. If the tribes are small, 40 feet will be sufficient for this activity.) Blindfold each tribe member using his or her bandana. Instruct each team member to put one hand on the rope. Explain that throughout the challenge, each member must keep one hand on the rope. The team will work together to form an equilateral triangle. They will be given two minutes to accomplish the task. The team that comes the closest to forming a triangle will win the challenge. The team that wins will receive their luggage as a reward.

❑ After the challenge, plan a reward activity for the entire group. This might be a bonfire with singing and fellowship, ice cream party, or pool party. Send each tribe back to its respective camp to sleep. Have an adult volunteer deliver luggage and supplies to whichever tribe didn't win the challenge.

❑ In the morning declare a merger among the tribes. After breakfast, take the group to perform a missions project with a ministry in town. A work project would be ideal. Have students paint, do lawn work, pick up trash, clean someone's house, etc.

Close the Session

❑ Complete the weekend with a time of worship, testimony, and celebration of all that the group has accomplished in the past year.

Ministry/Witnessing
Prayerwalking

Before the Session

❑ Plan a prayerwalking experience for the students to participate in during this session.

❑ If you hold your meeting in the evenings, plan to have several adult drivers. Drive students to several different locations to pray. Otherwise, plan a walking route that groups can follow.

❑ Be sure to inform your pastor and your students' parents of the prayerwalk.

❑ Prepare a map that each group will follow. The map will show where the students are to stop and what they are to pray for.

❑ Ask for adult volunteers to participate in the prayerwalk. Plan for one adult to accompany each group.

During the Session

❑ As students arrive, divide them into several small groups of three or four each. Assign an adult volunteer to each group. Give each group a map of where they are to go and pray. Inform students how much time they will have to go to their various stops and what time they are to meet back at the church to end their prayerwalk.

Example Locations

Go to the local fire department. Pray for:

• the work that firefighters do each day;

• the families that are affected by the devastation of fire;

• the families of firefighters, who worry about
• them when they are working.

Go to a local school. Pray for:

• your friends who are lost;

• the administration;

• teachers.

Go to a local "hang out" spot. Pray for:
- those who go there who don't know Jesus;
- safety of teenagers who go there;
- protection for the area.

Go to someone's house who you would like to see come to Youth on Mission℠ or to church. Pray for:
- the courage to invite the person to come;
- that the person's heart would be softened;
- that God would use you to minister to the needs of that person.

These are only some examples. Make up a different list for each group so that many areas of your community will be prayed over during the event.

Close the Session

❑ Have everyone who participated meet at the entrance of the church. Explain that you will end the session by prayerwalking in your church building. Take the students to different rooms in the church. Have students walk from room to room in silence. As you enter each room, ask students to hold hands and then call on one student to pray over the room and the ministry that goes on in the room. For example, in the youth Sunday School room, students can pray for the teachers, for students who they would like to see sitting in the room, for pure hearts of those who are members of the class, etc. End the prayerwalk in the sanctuary. Have students spread out around the room, and spend a few minutes in silent prayer. Close the session by singing a worship chorus, and then exit silently.

Cultural Experience
Celebrate a Year of Missions

Before the Session

❑ Decide on a time and date to hold a Youth on Mission celebration banquet. Reserve a location to hold the event.

❑ Invite a missionary speaker to share about his or her ministry during the event.

❑ Prepare a slide show of pictures from the ministry events of the past year.

❑ Ask the Women on Mission® group, Adults on Mission℠ team, or other adult missions group to prepare an ethnic meal for the students to enjoy.

❑ Decorate the meeting room in a festive manner.

❑ Send out invitations to community members and others who have been a part of ministry projects that were performed throughout the year.

During the Session

❑ As students and guests arrive, have festive music playing that goes with the theme of the decorations and food.

❑ Begin the evening with food and fellowship. After everyone has enjoyed the meal, serve dessert and coffee and introduce the missionary speaker for the evening. Use the following schedule for the rest of the evening:
- Introduction of speaker
- Missionary speaker
- Brief word from the leader about the accomplishments of the year
- Slide show
- Testimonies of students about the impact of the events of the last year on their lives.
- Leader presentations—The leader will present each student with some type of memento to remember the past year's ministry events. This might be a framed picture of the group during a missions project, a special letter of encouragement, or an award for crazy categories. Use this time to highlight the importance of each student and his or her contribution to the group.
- View of the future—Give students a taste of what is to come for the coming year. Play a game of 20 questions with them. Students are allowed to ask 20 yes or no questions to figure out the big event of the coming year. Reveal your preliminary plans for the coming year in a dramatic way.

Close the Session

❑ Close the evening in group prayer. Have everyone hold hands and ask a student to close in prayer.

Missionary Ministry
Cynthia White (Cape Town, South Africa)

Before the Session
- ❏ Plan to hold this session on a basketball court. Bring enough basketballs for each group of five to have one.
- ❏ Read through the story of Cynthia White (p. 88). Be prepared to tell her story in your own words.

During the Session
- ❏ As students arrive, divide them into groups of five. Give each group a basketball and divide them up between two basketball goals. Have each group play a game of Horse, but instead of spelling *horse,* have the teams spell *missions.* Each player will shoot the ball from anywhere on the half court. If the first player makes the shot, each of the other players must make the shot from the same position. If they do not make the shot, they get the first letter in the word *missions.* The group will continue to shoot baskets until one member has all the letters to spell *missions.* If the first person in the group misses his or her shot, each person continues to take a shot until someone makes a basket.
- ❏ After each group has finished, gather everyone together for the missionary story. Tell the story of Cynthia White.

Close the Session
- ❏ Have students stand in a circle. Bounce a basketball to someone in the circle. The person who catches the basketball must lead in a short prayer for Cynthia and the work that she does in Cape Town. Continue to bounce the basketball to several students. Ask each one to lead in a short prayer for some aspect of Cynthia's ministry.

Cynthia White
Cape Town, South Africa

Cynthia White is a missionary who serves in Cape Town, South Africa. Since she was a child, Cynthia has been involved in sports. In high school and in junior college, she played basketball and softball. She never imagined she would be able to use her love for sports in ministry!

After college, Cynthia attended seminary. It was at that time that she had the opportunity to serve with an organization called International Sports Federation (ISF). ISF is an organization that sends sports teams overseas to work alongside missionaries. Teams use a specific sport to reach people through clinics, practices, and games. The athletes also use the opportunity to share their testimonies about Christ. During one of Cynthia's trips to Cape Town, South Africa, she felt God calling her to the area to serve through sports evangelism. God was faithful to her call, and in June 2000, Cynthia became a full-time missionary in South Africa.

Cynthia works in Mitchells Plain, a poor area of South Africa. The schools in the area do not have basketball teams, so Cynthia uses basketball as a way to get into the schools. She works with teachers and students and teaches them how to play the sport of basketball. Through this, she is able to share her testimony and share the reason why she moved to South Africa from America.

Extra Pages

Contacts for Missions Trip Ideas

The following offices provide opportunities for youth missions projects. Contact them with your questions regarding a missions trip for your youth:

• WMU Volunteer Connection
• State WMU Office
• State Partnership Missions Office
• North American Mission Board Student Missions Office
• International Mission Board Youth Volunteer Office
• LifeWay Christian Resources, M-Fuge

Opportunities include one- and two-week projects in North America and around the world; and four- to ten-week service opportunities at summer camps and community Centers and churches; among other things.

Also, to find out how a student in junior high, senior high, or college can be commissioned, recognized, and sent out by his/her local church to serve as a missionary on his/her campus, check out the student Web site www.studentz.com.

North American Mission Study for Youth

Every year in the month of March, youth have the opportunity to take part in a North American Mission Study.

Through your church WMU director or other appropriate staff person, secure the materials for the North American Mission Study for youth. Set aside a time for the youth to do their study.

Work with your church staff and WMU leadership to find ways your youth can participate in the churchwide observance of the Week of Prayer for North American Missions. They can participate in worship services by sharing facts about missionaries or doing dramatic/music presentations about missions. Be sure to have youth participate in the offering, setting a giving goal.

International Mission Study for Youth

Every year during the Christmas season, youth have the opportunity to take part in the International Mission Study.

Through your church WMU director or a staff person, secure the materials for the International Mission Study for youth. Plan a time for the youth to do their study. You may want to hold it during a lock-in or a weekend retreat.

Work with your church staff and WMU director to find ways youth can participate in the churchwide observance of the Week of Prayer for International Missions. Consider adopting an unreached people group for the coming year. Your youth might want to participate in worship services throughout the month of November by giving a "missions moment" to highlight different missionaries. The youth can also be called on to lead in prayer during the emphasis. Have youth participate in the offering. Set a goal for just the youth group.

Helpful Addresses and Web Sites

Woman's Missionary Union
P. O. Box 830010
Birmingham, AL 35283-0010
(205) 991-8100
Customer Service: 1-800-968-7301
www.wmu.com
www.wmustore.com
www.acteens.com
www.missionsinterchange.com

Volunteer Connection
P. O. Box 830010
Birmingham, AL 35283-0010
(205) 991-4097
volconnection@wmu.org
www.wmu.com—click on Ministry Opportunities

North American Mission Board
4200 North Point Parkway
Alpharetta, GA 30022-4176
(770) 410-6000
1-800-462-VOLS
www.namb.net
www.studentz.com

International Mission Board
P. O. Box 6767
Richmond, VA 23230-0767
1-800-866-3621
www.imb.org
www.thetask.org

Ethics and Religious Liberty Commission
901 Commerce Street, #550
Nashville, TN 37203-3696
(615) 244-2495
www.erlc.com
www.beathunger.com

LifeWay Christian Resources
127 Ninth Avenue North
Nashville, TN 37234-0113
(615) 251-2000
www.lifeway.com

Ministries

Volunteer Connection^{SM}
Volunteer Connection is a ministry that connects missions volunteers to needs, nationally and internationally. A missions volunteer is any Christian who has chosen to give their time, skills, and resources to meet a need in a mission setting. Volunteer Connection encourages volunteers to complete a simple, user-friendly training program, so they will be better qualified to serve.

Join hundreds of Christ followers as a missions volunteer by participating in FamilyFEST and/or MissionsFEST. Volunteers do projects such as:
Light Construction
Landscaping
Repairs
VBS
Health Fairs
Sports Camps
Prayerwalking
Servant Evangelism
Bible Clubs

FamilyFEST is open to anyone first grade and older. Perfect for families, adult teams, and student teams. MissionsFEST is open to men and women 18 years of age and older.

Pure Water, Pure Love^{SM}
Pure Water, Pure Love is a WMU ministry to provide missionaries overseas with a water purifier that will remove disease-causing microorganisms. Individuals, churches, Sunday Schools, missions groups, etc. can give money to purchase a water purifier that will provide enough drinking water for four years.

Anyone can be a part of Pure Water, Pure Love through their donation to WMU. For an average of $250, water treatment supplies can make a world of difference to a missionary. Filters and/or treatment kits are supplied to missionaries at no charge.

Collect money from your church, your youth group, your friends, or your family. Or make a personal donation. Please be sure and let us know to whom to send the gift acknowledgement. Send a check made out to WMU and clearly marked for PWPL, to:

PWPL
c/o WMU
P. O. Box 830010
Birmingham, AL 35283-0010

If you have additional questions, please email purewater@wmu.org or call Barbara Yeager at (205) 991-4091.

**International
Initiatives**^{SM}

International
Initiatives exists to
provide men and
women with the
opportunity to be a
part of international
missions. The goal
is to move beyond
our personal lives
and circumstances
to impact a new and
different area for Christ. For many, the idea of an
international missions trip is overwhelming.
International Initiatives seeks to remove the overwhelming obstacles so that you can freely use who
you are to minister to others in the name of Jesus
Christ.

In 2004, we continued our partnerships with
France, Greece, and Croatia. As we turn our attention to the Balkan area and as plans are unveiled
for Project HELP^{SM}: Poverty, search your heart for
how God is leading you, your church, your family
to impact the world. For more information on mission opportunities through national WMU, please
contact Jean Cullen at jcullen@wmu.org.

WorldCrafts

WorldCrafts^{SM}

WorldCrafts is a WMU nonprofit ministry that
imports handcrafts from around the world and
markets them in the US. Most items are made by
men and women living in poverty; the income
from these crafts helps them better provide for
their families through their skills. WorldCrafts
items are fairly traded items, which means they
are produced in nonexploitative conditions by
artisans who are paid a fair wage.

WorldCrafts is a collection of unique and beautiful
handmade items from around the world, including
items from Liberia, Tanzania, China, Jordan,
Thailand, India, Chile, South Africa, Turkey, and
Pakistan.

When you purchase WorldCrafts, you join with
other caring people to provide income, improved
self-esteem, and hope to people from around the
world. So for your next gift-giving occasion, buy
WorldCrafts—gifts that will mean the world to
them!

Exciting Re

The BIG BOOK of Ministry Ideas for Students
Sarah S. Groves

This is a must-have for every missions-minded leader who works with students. It's chock-full of hands-on ministry ideas, including tips for planning a missions trip.
W036104, $9.99

Growing Godly Women: A Christian Woman's Guide to Mentoring Teenage Girls
Donna Margaret Greene

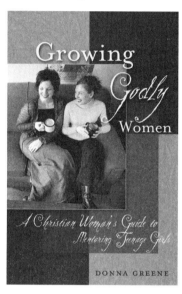

Growing Godly Women is a blueprint for making a vital difference in a girl's life through a mentoring relationship, providing her with crucial support and wisdom during the complex teen years.
N034107, $9.99

A Girl's Life with God
Casey Hartley Gibbons

Former Miss American Teen, Casey Hartley Gibbons, leads teen girls to find God's richest gifts by giving their thoughts, actions, and relationships to Him.
N034115, $8.99

In Daily Pursuit: Following Christ for Life
Judi S. Hayes

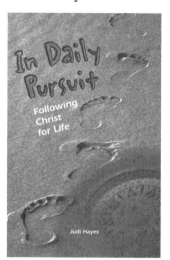

This daily guide challenges Christian teenagers to understand and utilize their spiritual disciplines through focusing on biblical and modern-day examples.
W046103, $8.99

To order, call 1-800-968-7301 or
visit us online at www.wmustore.com.

Youth Resources

Letters from Campus: College Girls' Insights for High School Graduates

Donna Margaret Greene

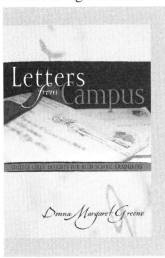

Written from college girls to girls graduating from high school, these letters offer the inside scoop on what concerns graduates most, including getting ready for college, leaving home, and relying on God. N034114, $9.99

ChristLight: Reflecting the Image of Christ in the Real World

Janet Hoffman

Contains 40 daily devotions written especially for

teenaged girls. What a great way for leaders to encourage spiritual development in their girls in areas such as prayer, Bible study, and stewardship. W036103, $9.99

Youth on Mission

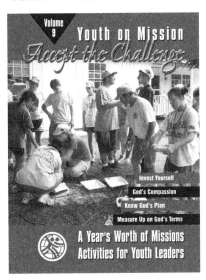

Need to spice up your youth program with a missions element designed just for teenagers? These resources provide leaders with a year's worth of plans to help youth develop the outward focus that God intends for our Christian lives. Complete with an introductory How-To section, they outline all that an adult leader needs to know to use the material. Each of the 12 units includes a missions Bible study, a group learning activity, a missions project idea, and other features. This flexible resource can be used to add a missions component to ongoing youth programs or as a more specialized youth missions organization.

Youth on Mission: *Accept the Challenge*, vol. 9
Judi S. Hayes
W036101, $15.99

Youth on Mission: *God's Plan…My Part*, vol. 8
Tim and Janet Bearden
W026101, $15.99

To order, shop online at www.wmustore.com or call 1-800-968-7301.

Exciting

Missions on Stage: Dramas, Skits, and Choruses

Karen Anderson Holcomb

This book provides a variety of ways to creatively stage all types of missions presentations; includes responsive readings, sample commissioning services, mission skits, and more!

W044136, $10.99
Available January 2005

Music for Missions: WMU Music CD

Finding just the right music for your mission studies, emphases, and commissionings will never be easier with your purchase of *Music for Missions*. Contains both vocal and accompaniment tracks.

W043117, $14.99

She Walked with Jesus: Stories of Christ Followers in the Bible

Brenda Poinsett

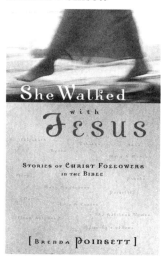

This book focuses on the "good women" of the New Testament, Christ followers who used their gifts and abilities in Jesus' service. These stories will encourage those unsung heroes, the women who support the work of Christ's church today.

N044103, $9.99

The Story of Annie Armstrong

Cathy Butler

The life of Annie Armstrong is examined as she begins a missions movement in the United States in the early twentieth century.

W043106, $9.99

The Story of Lottie Moon
Deena Newman

The life of Lottie Moon is examined as she begins a missions movement in China in the late nineteenth and early twentieth centuries.

W043107, $9.99

Using Crafts in Ministry
Linda and Jackie Hutto

In this excellent how-to crafts book, find creative craft ideas, patterns, and instructions for making crafts suitable for use in ministry and missions opportunities. It is appropriate for all skill levels.

W004102, $8.99

To order, shop online at www.wmustore.com or call 1-800-968-7301.

Graduating Seniors

You've spent years investing in their lives. With your help, they've learned about missions in your own hometown and halfway around the world. You've watched them grow through hands-on ministry opportunities. Now that they're graduating, send them off into the "real world" prepared, with www.missionsinterchange.com.

Missions Interchange is the only missions Web site designed specifically for collegiate women. Are your graduates interested in learning how to share their faith, understand Muslims, or reach out to international students? How about tips on "real life" topics like dating, roommates, and careers? They'll find all this, and much more, at www.missionsinterchange.com.

www.missionsinterchange.com

missions interchange

helping collegiate women discover
the joy of missions